Inventive Minds

Inventive Minds

Marvin Minsky on Education

Edited by Cynthia Solomon and Xiao Xiao
Illustrated by Xiao Xiao

The MIT Press
Cambridge, Massachusetts
London, England

The MIT Press
Massachusetts Institute of Technology
77 Massachusetts Avenue, Cambridge, MA 02139
mitpress.mit.edu

© 2019 Massachusetts Institute of Technology

All rights reserved. No part of this book may be reproduced in any form by any electronic or mechanical means (including photocopying, recording, or information storage and retrieval) without permission in writing from the publisher.

This book was set in ITC Stone Serif Std by Toppan Best-set Premedia Limited.

Library of Congress Cataloging-in-Publication Data

Names: Minsky, Marvin, 1927-2016, author. | Solomon, Cynthia, editor. | Xiao, Xiao, editor.
Title: Inventive minds : Marvin Minsky on education / Marvin Minsky ; edited by Cynthia Solomon and Xiao Xiao ; illustrated by Xiao Xiao.
Description: Cambridge, MA : MIT Press, [2018] | Includes bibliographical references and index.
Identifiers: LCCN 2018011627 | ISBN 9780262039093 (hardcover : alk. paper), 9780262052931 (paperback)
Subjects: LCSH: Critical thinking--Study and teaching. | Thought and thinking--Study and teaching. | Learning, Psychology of. | Minsky, Marvin, 1927-2016
Classification: LCC LB1590.3 .M555 2018 | DDC 370.15/2--dc23 LC record available at https://lccn.loc.gov/2018011627

151257765

Contents

Acknowledgments   vii
A Short Biography of Marvin Minsky   xi
Preface by Cynthia Solomon   xv
Introduction by Mike Travers   xxix

Essays by Marvin Minsky

1   The Infinite Construction Kit   3
Afterword to Essay 1 by Alan Kay   19

Introductory Remarks to Essay 2 by Hal Abelson   37
2   What Makes Mathematics Hard to Learn?   41

Introductory Remarks to Essay 3 by Gary Stager   59
3   Effects of Grade-Based Segregation   65

Introductory Remarks to Essay 4 by Brian Silverman   77
4   Learning from Role Models, Mentors, and Imprimers   81

Introductory Remarks to Essay 5 by Walter Bender   99
5   Questioning General Education   103

Introductory Remarks to Essay 6 by Patrick Henry Winston   121
6   Education and Psychology   127

Afterword by Margaret Minsky   155

Contributors   163
Notes   167
Further Reading   177
Index   181

Acknowledgments

We are immensely grateful to Marvin Minsky for writing his thoughts on children and education. We are also grateful for Seymour Papert and his collaboration with Marvin.

This book would not have happened without the input and support of Gloria Rudisch and Margaret Minsky. Gloria, a pediatrician and public health practitioner, was also Marvin's wife. She was extraordinarily helpful as the book slowly came together. She graciously allowed us to work from the Minsky home in Brookline, Massachusetts, and was always ready to read and offer feedback on our drafts. Margaret, our close colleague and friend, is also Marvin's elder daughter. Deeply familiar with her father's work and life, Margaret has been an invaluable resource and sounding board throughout this project.

We are greatly indebted to all our contributors: Mike Travers, Alan Kay, Hal Abelson, Gary Stager, Brian Silverman, Walter Bender, Patrick Winston, and Margaret Minsky. Thanks to their understanding and appreciation of Marvin, each of their essays brought out new facets of Marvin's words.

Cynthia thanks several people who played major roles in this project. Artemis Papert and Brian Silverman were critics, editors, and cheerleaders, as were Derek Breen, Allison Druin, and Dylan

Holmes. Anna Cullen-Voyatzakis, Belinda Berman-Real, Sandra Avola, and Sherry Thompson were also extremely supportive and encouraging.

Xiao gives special thanks to Idit Harel for her advice, encouragement, and anecdotes. Many of Xiao's own views on the art of learning came from interactions and conversations with Donal Fox and the late Edith Ackermann. Insights from Donal on music learning inspired several illustrations in essay 5. Xiao is grateful to her former advisor, Hiroshi Ishii, for the freedom to explore her interest in learning in her doctoral thesis, and for the appointment of Research Affiliate at the MIT Media Lab while working on this book. Xiao also thanks Danbee Kim, DonDerek Haddad, and Briana Eden for their suggestions, motivation, and loving support.

We thank our families—for Cynthia: Erric Solomon, Jon Solomon, Eva Hopf, Sandi Slone, Bruce Ehrmann, and Luwen Solomon, and for Xiao: Xiaocheng Wu, Ke Xiao, Yongji Li, Xianda Wu, Xiaomei Wu, Jianghai Han, and Andy Han.

We also thank the Minsky extended family—Richard Amster, who was an invaluable resource in helping us review our book contract; the Minsky grandchildren, Miles Steele, Charlotte Minsky, Gigi Minsky, and Harry Minsky, each an inventive mind and all an inspiration; and other Minsky family members including Oliver Steele, Julie Minsky, Lance Rushing, Henry Minsky, Milan Minsky, Richard Amster, and Ruth Amster for their support.

This book is part of a broader effort led by Margaret Minsky to archive Marvin's life and work. Others who have been involved in that effort include Yoshiki Ohshima, Brian Bradley, Richard Amster, Teresa Marrin Nakra, Paula Aguilera, Jonathan Williams, Ruben Marques, and Rodrigo Santos. Their work has been an invaluable resource for us. Heikke Ruuska has also been very helpful.

Acknowledgments

Many thanks to Mel King and Susan Klimczak at the South End Technology Center for hosting several of our work sessions. In particular, we thank David Cavallo for his reminders of Seymour, Ed Baffi for his input on titles, and Harlem Cruz for equipping us with a workspace.

Last but not least, we thank Susan Buckley and Noah Springer at the MIT Press and Chris Bourg at the MIT Libraries for their belief in the value of Marvin's ideas on learning and education. We are deeply grateful for their support in bringing this book to life.

A Short Biography of Marvin Minsky

Marvin Minsky was Toshiba Professor of Media Arts and Sciences and Professor of Electrical Engineering and Computer Science at the Massachusetts Institute of Technology. His research has led to both theoretical and practical advances in artificial intelligence, cognitive science, neural networks, and the theory of Turing Machines and recursive functions. He made other contributions in the domains of graphics, symbolic mathematical computation, knowledge representation, commonsensical semantics, machine perception, and both symbolic and connectionist learning.

Professor Minsky was a pioneer in robotics and telepresence. He designed and built mechanical arms, hands with tactile sensors, and one of the first Logo "turtles." These influenced many subsequent robotic projects. He was also involved with advanced technologies for exploring space and was a consultant on Stanley Kubrick's *2001: A Space Odyssey*.

In 1951, he built the first randomly wired neural network learning machine (called SNARC, for Stochastic Neural-Analog Reinforcement Computer), based on reinforcing synaptic connections. In 1956, when a Junior Fellow at Harvard, he invented and built the first Confocal Scanning Microscope, an optical instrument with unprecedented resolution and image quality.

After the early 1950s, Minsky worked on using computational ideas to characterize human psychological processes, and also on endowing machines with intelligence. In the early 1970s, he and Seymour Papert began formulating a theory called the Society of Mind that combined insights from developmental child psychology and their experience with research on artificial intelligence. The Society of Mind proposes that intelligence is not the product of any singular mechanism but comes from the managed interaction of a diverse variety of resourceful agents.

In 1985, Minsky published *The Society of Mind*, a book in which 270 interconnected one-page ideas reflect the structure of the theory itself. In 2006, he published a sequel, *The Emotion Machine*, which proposes theories that could account for human higher-level feelings, goals, emotions, and conscious thoughts in terms of multiple levels of processes, some of which can reflect on the others. By providing us with multiple different "ways to think," these processes might account for much of our uniquely human resourcefulness.

In addition to his technical achievements, Marvin was an accomplished classical pianist. He taught himself to improvise in the style of Bach and Beethoven, and continued to play until his death on January 24, 2016.

Marvin's own formal schooling played an important role throughout his life, and so we list it here.

The Fieldston School, New York

Bronx High School of Science, New York

Phillips Academy, Andover, Massachusetts

United States Navy, 1944–1945

B.A. Mathematics, Harvard University, 1946–1950

Ph.D. Mathematics, Princeton University, 1951–1954

Junior Fellow, Harvard Society of Fellows, 1954–1957

Preface

Cynthia Solomon

> Computer Science is not only about computers themselves; more generally, it provides us with a whole new world of ways to understand complex processes—including the ones that go on in our own mind. For until those new techniques arrived (such as programming languages for describing processes, and data structures for representing knowledge), we had no expressions that people could use to articulate—and then communicate—good new ideas about such things.
>
> —Marvin Minsky[1]

Marvin Minsky is known worldwide as a cofounder of the field of artificial intelligence (AI). For Marvin, AI was not about creating machines with only the surface appearance of intelligent behavior. He was interested in making machines that mimic how humans think. At heart, Marvin's vision for AI was always a quest to unravel and understand the mysterious mechanisms behind the human mind. His books *The Society of Mind* and *The Emotion Machine* proposed elegant theories explaining the diverse dimensions of human thinking including common sense, emotions, perception, action, and how thinking evolves in an individual over time.[2]

Marvin's insights about the mind are relevant not only for creating intelligent machines, but also for providing new perspectives on children's learning and thinking, as well as on the role of computers, both in education and in schools. These are the topics explored by the essays in this book.

Marvin Minsky and Seymour Papert

When I think about children I cannot help but think about Seymour Papert and his statement that "you can't think about thinking without thinking about thinking about something."[3] Known for his pioneering work in bringing computers to children and rethinking school, Seymour was a close colleague of Marvin's for many years. They codirected the Artificial Intelligence Laboratory at MIT, collaborated on countless projects, and co-advised many students in both the MIT AI Lab and the MIT Media Lab.

In reading the essays in this book I am reminded of how much Marvin and Seymour thought alike. A kind of proof is in the story of how they met at a conference in England in the summer of 1960. Without prior knowledge they gave almost identical papers—on learning in random nets. Their shared outlooks resonated throughout their work both together and individually over the next forty years.

This similarity in thinking may not be obvious for those who did not know the two personally. They both thought about using computers to make artificial intelligence and also to enhance people's learning and ways of thinking. Even though both of them were fascinated by the mind and by learning, their priorities differed. Marvin's goal was to create machines that could think like people while Seymour focused on machines as a

Preface

Marvin Minsky (left) and Seymour Papert (right)

means to empower children to think about their own thinking. This collection of essays illustrates their overlapping interests in learning and education.

In a nutshell, Seymour's writings concentrated on the "outside" (e.g., schools, social situations, environments) while Marvin's centered on the "inside" mechanisms of the mind. This difference can be traced in part to their imprimers. For Marvin it was Freud, whom Marvin saw as the first person in history to have theories of mind that one could work with, whether they were right or wrong: there are different parts of the mind and executive systems for managing them. For Seymour it was Piaget, who showed that children are not empty vessels. For Piaget, children have theories that are different from those of adults but, with age and experience, their theories change. Both Marvin and Seymour shared a view that Marvin summed up in what he called "Papert's principle," which encapsulates Seymour's interpretation of Piaget's work with children and fits in with Freud's analysis that there are executive systems for managing different parts of the mind:

> **Papert's Principle:** *Some of the most crucial steps in mental growth are based not on simply acquiring new skills, but on acquiring new administrative ways to use what one already knows.*[4]

Papert's principle illustrates how Marvin and Seymour complemented each other's thinking. Though Seymour did think about the "inside" workings of the mind, he focused on finding real-life examples of situations with people to support his ideas. Marvin was the one to formulate this idea as a general principle, and Marvin was constantly trying to explain and verify principles he found by writing programs in his head to simulate situations and experiences.

Marvin's love for building machines extended into Seymour's work with children. He built a custom computer to run the Logo programming language and animated graphics, as well as a computer-controlled four-voice music box for children to experiment with sound in Logo. Although Marvin did not directly conduct research on school and learning, he did care about children's learning. The incredible insights shared in these essays provide a complementary perspective to Seymour's existing writings.

Marvin, Seymour, Me, Children, and Computers

I first met Marvin in the fall of 1962 when he was the director of the MIT Artificial Intelligence Group. John McCarthy had just left to direct the Stanford AI Lab. I wanted to learn to program, and being a woman of the time, I became Marvin's secretary. Marvin, his students, and the lab's hackers taught me about computers, programming languages, and controversies. I also learned a bit of Lisp, the lab's programming language developed by John McCarthy. I left the lab to program and in 1966 joined Bolt, Beranek and Newman (now BBN Technologies) to work in Wally Feurzeig's education group. Seymour was already consulting with Wally.

Seymour Papert, a South African, arrived at MIT in late 1963 after working with Jean Piaget in Geneva, Switzerland. Piaget, the famous genetic epistemologist, showed that children have their own theories about their world. These theories are shaped and changed as children gain knowledge and experience, and as they apply Papert's principle. With the help of Warren McCulloch, the great cyberneticist, Marvin arranged for Seymour to join the MIT community. Thus began the long and rich collaboration between Marvin and Seymour.

I collaborated with both Marvin and Seymour on uses of computers in education. Along with Seymour, I was one of the original designers of Logo, the first programming language created for children. Logo started in the late 60s, and was originally a text-only system. Children manipulated words and sentences to make games, stories, and teaching programs. In 1968–1969, Seymour and I taught seventh graders computer math instead of their regular math course.

After the 1968–1969 school year, we started the Logo Group as part of the MIT AI Lab. At the same time, Seymour declared that children needed more concrete objects than words and sentences to think with. Thus turtles were born, both physical and graphical. We called them "floor" and "display" turtles,

Seymour Papert and Cynthia Solomon

respectively. Marvin was involved in the creation of the first floor turtle and built the music box controlled through Logo.

In 1970–1971, Seymour and I taught fifth graders. We had a new version of Logo that talked to a "display turtle," a "floor turtle," and Marvin's music box. Kids could compute, write, make line drawings, animate, and make music. By 1972, the lab built a completely new Logo environment on a time-shared Digital

Preface

Cynthia Solomon teaches Logo

Equipment Corporation (DEC) PDP-11 with turtle-graphics terminal stations.

We ran into trouble with the cost of the hardware and its scarcity, so in 1972, we started a company called General Turtle to make our own turtles and music boxes. Marvin got the idea of making a Logo turtle-graphics computer. The 2500, as it was called, used vector graphics and provided a new extension to turtle graphics. By this time it was the mid-70s, when the Altair and a new generation of standalone desktop computers were coming into being.

The next time Marvin, Seymour, and I (along with a couple of other people) formed a company was in 1980. Logo Computer Systems' first job was to make a Logo for the Apple II Computer. I directed the group, most of whom had been part of the Logo Group at MIT. I also wrote an introductory book for turtle graphics.

Marvin and Me

My next step was to start the Atari Cambridge Research Lab under the aegis of Alan Kay. The Boston office of Logo Computer Systems closed and most of those folks joined me at Atari where we were building the *PlayStation of the future*. This core contingent of Logo employees had been part of the push to make Apple Logo commercially available. That job done, we were now free to rethink the language and its environment. Marvin was our major advisor.

Most of this group had a shared history of collaborating with each other, and with both Marvin and Seymour. We had a vision of building a new object-oriented Logo with modules for color vector-graphics, animation, and music construction. We experimented with peripherals such as a force-feedback joystick and created one of the earliest force-sensing screens.

Logo Computer Systems in Montreal made a commercial version of Logo for the Atari computer. Margaret Minsky and I decided to publish a growing collection of interesting Atari Logo programming projects created by our friends, and Marvin wrote a preface.[5] It is essay 1 in this book.

Preface

The Atari Lab, as glorious and productive as it was, only lasted about two years, and closed just as the MIT Media Lab opened. Marvin and Seymour were two of the founding faculty of the Media Lab.

I followed a different path, finishing up my doctorate and teaching children. Several years later, Marvin and I rejoined our efforts with children and computing through One Laptop per Child (OLPC), which was an ambitious project founded by Nicholas Negroponte, Seymour, and partners. Its mission was to empower children in developing countries to learn by providing laptops to every school-age child. One of Marvin's contributions to OLPC was a series of essays on education. They are essays 2 through 6 in this book.

How This Book Came About

Marvin had posted his writing on his website. Most were published elsewhere, but these essays on education were released in now-defunct media. The book containing essay 1 is now out of print. Essays 2 through 6, written for One Laptop per Child, were not widely publicized. Given the new wave of interest in computer science education, these essays are more relevant than ever. I invited a group of leading thinkers in their fields to comment on Marvin's essays. Some are educators, others are pioneering researchers in computing and AI, and all knew Marvin well. Here are the people I chose to comment on each of the essays:

Alan Kay met Marvin in 1968 and was captivated by Seymour and Marvin's thoughts on children's learning. That year he also visited the seventh grade Logo math class Seymour and I taught. In 1970 as he began work on Smalltalk, the Alto, and the Dynabook at Xerox PARC, he visited us again observing fifth graders programming floor and display turtles and making music. His Smalltalk world would include graphics, animation, music, debugging aids, and editors for children.

As Chief Scientist at Atari, Inc., Alan asked me to set up the Atari Cambridge Research Lab near MIT in 1982. When the Atari Lab closed in 1984, Alan and three staffers became part of the just-forming MIT Media Lab, where Marvin and Seymour were part of the founding faculty.

Hal Abelson joined the MIT AI Lab's Logo Group when it was first formed in 1969 and was a major contributor to the development of turtles and turtle geometry. As a professor he and Gerry Sussman, one of Marvin's outstanding undergraduate and graduate students, developed the introductory MIT programming course 6.001. As part of the AI Lab, Hal influenced and was influenced by Marvin.

Gary Stager is a wonderful outspoken advocate for children. He has been a major contributor to the Logo community since the early 1980s through his writings and workshops. He worked closely with Seymour and was one of the main teachers in Seymour's Maine juvenile jail project. There, his students' projects included a range of programming projects, self-reflective writing, and robotics. His Constructing Modern Knowledge summer workshop was held for the tenth consecutive year in July 2017. Marvin participated in the first eight workshops where participants spent an evening at the MIT Media Lab and an hour with Marvin asking him questions on an open range of topics.

Brian Silverman, as an undergraduate at MIT, built with Danny Hillis a tic-tac-toe computer out of Tinkertoy parts. Along with Danny, Margaret Minsky, and other MIT classmates, he had several discussions about this book with Marvin. In the late 1970s,

Brian became deeply involved in Logo research and development. As the major programmer at Logo Computer Systems Inc., he was responsible for several versions of Logo, including Atari Logo, LogoWriter, and MicroWorlds. He worked closely with Seymour and collaborates with Mitchel Resnick on Scratch and assorted hardware projects. He and Paula Bontá created TurtleArt and with Artemis Papert have promoted it as an artistic and expressive medium.

Walter Bender knew Marvin personally as well as from his writing. Walter was part of Nicholas Negroponte's ArcMac Group preceding the Media Lab. He eventually became director of the Media Lab and then coordinated the One Laptop per Child enterprise for a few years. He thus came to know Marvin well and to work with him. It was Walter who encouraged Marvin to write some of these essays for One Laptop per Child.

I knew **Patrick H. Winston** had a special rapport with Marvin even when he was a student. For example, Patrick knew instinctually something that most of us had to learn later about Marvin. Marvin didn't like sitting for long and often in the midst of a conversation would get up and walk out of his office or whatever room he was in. Some people thought Marvin had deserted them and sat befuddled waiting for him to return. Patrick did not sit still but got up and accompanied Marvin. When Patrick was Marvin's graduate student he would joke that if you wanted to get a thesis done, just follow Marvin around. He did, and he did. Patrick's introductory AI course served as a feeder to Marvin's AI seminar. When Marvin stepped down as director of the AI Lab, Patrick took on the position for several years and his Genesis Project research on story understanding has been a significant continuation of important AI work and builds on Marvin's theories.

I asked **Mike Travers**, a former Media Lab graduate student under Marvin, to write the introduction. On his blog, he had published a beautiful essay on Marvin immediately after news of Marvin's death.[6] Mike's writing let me feel Marvin's presence, and he does not disappoint in his introduction to these essays.

Margaret Minsky, Marvin's daughter, played an essential behind-the-scenes role in the development of this book. She enthusiastically endorsed the project and was always available for critiques and edits. Her afterword reflects her deep understanding of Marvin and his thinking not only as an AI researcher and teacher but also as a musician and family man.

In her early research career, Margaret was a vital member of the MIT AI Lab's Logo Group, Logo Computer Systems, Inc., and the Atari Cambridge Research Lab, where she worked with several other contributors to this book. She brought much of that culture to her research in creating haptic interfaces and is now engaged in creating multimedia artifacts exploring learning, improvisation, and thought. Her recent investigations concern embodied interaction with technology aimed at increasing cognitive, social, and physical well-being.

Xiao Xiao started out as the book's illustrator and later became a very necessary coeditor. She was a graduate student at the MIT Media Lab when she developed a working relationship with Marvin. Xiao had created a system for the piano that gave the illusion of a virtual reflection playing the physical instrument, and Marvin was one of the featured players. Xiao had attended a few salon meetings in Marvin's living room. Later, she was a weekly guest at the Minsky home, playing the piano for and with Marvin. I had caught her drawing in a sketchbook while in his living room, and so I enticed her to illustrate this book.

Marvin and Education

In these six essays, Marvin shares his wisdom about children, learning, school, and computation. He emphasizes computers not only as tools for learning typical subject areas like math but also as offering opportunities for children to learn *"good ways to think about thinking"* itself. One way of doing this, Marvin suggests, is "to get children to think of themselves as though they were programmed computers" (essay 4). For instance, in my Logo classes children were asked to "play turtle" or to become researchers collecting both computer and human bugs, to talk about necessary debugging steps, and at times to recognize that some bugs can be features.

Another one of Marvin's ever-sharp observations is about teaching: "instead of promoting inventiveness, we focus on preventing mistakes." In teaching children arithmetic, he suspected that "this negative emphasis leads many children not only to dislike Arithmetic, but also later to become averse to everything else that smells of technology (essay 2).

Unsurprisingly, these essays are relevant to today's discussions about school, computers, and learning. I assume most readers have thought about the issues raised here; Marvin adds a refreshing perspective. We leave it to you to bring in your knowledge of other writers and researchers offering similar, or contrary, points of view. Enjoy Marvin's wisdom.

Introduction

Mike Travers

> When your ideas seem inadequate, remember someone more expert at this, and imagine what that person would do.
> —Marvin Minsky (Essay 4)

We have some preconceived ideas about genius—that it is a divine mystery, a gift given to just a few, something both inexplicable and inaccessible to ordinary people. Marvin Minsky was a recognized genius, but it was the nature of his particular form of genius to question the very idea of innate talent and aptitude and the mystifications that surround it. To Marvin, the idea that the mind (or anything else) was beyond explanation was an affront and a challenge.

Marvin was brilliant in numerous ways aside from the work on artificial intelligence for which he is best known: he was an accomplished inventor, mathematician, and musician. But his big trick was to face squarely the mechanical nature of the human mind and not be alarmed by it. Indeed, he found it rather delightful and intriguing. This put him at odds with standard-issue humanists, which suited him just fine. But Marvin himself was not in any way inhuman, far from it. He was an extremely warm and welcoming individual, and always willing to engage with anyone's open mind. For example, he was active in Usenet discussion groups (chiefly comp.ai.philosophy), where he would explain or argue his views on AI with all comers regardless of their academic qualifications.

Marvin had a unique talent for reflecting on mental processes and coming up with plausible mechanisms that might explain how they worked. He applied this ability to his own mind, of course, but also to the thinking of his students, mentors, colleagues, and friends. He delighted in the cleverness of mental machinery, and sought to understand it by modeling it and encouraging others to share in the task of self-understanding.

Minsky is usually identified with computer technology and artificial intelligence, but there is little in the following essays that is specifically about digital technology or, indeed, technology of any sort. Their focus is on the psychology of learning, and the nature of systems that are capable of learning. He hoped to build computers along these lines, but his inspiration was the human mind, and these essays are both reflections on how minds work and concrete suggestions for ways to reorganize education to better support them—in some cases by involving the intelligent deployment of computer technology, to be sure, but never as the central focus. Technology is merely a tool in pursuit of better understandings, and computer programming merely the best available language for expressing new ideas about how minds work.

Minsky's last two books, *Society of Mind* (SOM) and *The Emotion Machine* (TEM), were both crammed with simple, concrete, and powerful ideas for how minds—both natural and artificial— might be constructed, distilled from decades of work building computational models and guiding the work of others. Both were essentially technical books written in nontechnical language—

Introduction

a choice that may have caused some problems with their reception, as people did not quite know how to read them. But in this and in many other ways, Marvin gleefully ignored the standard boundaries and rules.

Situating These Essays

Five of the essays collected here emerged from Marvin's participation in the One Laptop per Child (OLPC) project, a massive effort to put computational technology in the hands of the world's children.[1] Marvin saw this as an opportunity to fix some of the ingrained bad habits of the educational system. For instance, essay 5 opens with the suggestion that the educational focus on broad general education is misplaced, and children would be better served by a system that allowed them to specialize and dive into a single topic they cared about deeply.

Regardless of the practicality of this idea, it's notable in what it indicates about his approach to learning. To Marvin, students were not empty vessels to be filled with knowledge, nor poor approximations of fully developed adults, but instead understood as fully active agents and creators of their own minds. As such, they needed to hone their mental skills on the kind of demanding tasks that come with intense pursuit of some personal goal. Traditional education provides content, but creators require methods and tools.

Marvin was finely attuned to the power of ideas, both good and bad, and the OLPC project was a chance *"to provide our children with ideas they could use to invent their own theories about themselves"* (essay 6). This was a call for a model of education entirely in tune with the ancient Greek injunction to "know thyself." Marvin saw that computers and computational ideas have the potential to give us much better tools for accomplishing this task than have ever existed before in history. The computational revolution in human self-knowledge has been enabled but not yet realized, and these essays may be considered efforts to move us toward that goal.

Themes

Marvin's thinking revolved around a number of tightly interconnected ideas, which pop up repeatedly in his writing here and elsewhere. Here I try to pull out and summarize a few of his most important recurring themes.

The Centrality of Goals

> We need to develop better ways to answer the questions that kids are afraid to ask, like *"What am I doing here, and why?"*
> —Marvin Minsky (Essay 2)

> You're almost always pursuing goals.
> —Marvin Minsky (Essay 4)

The importance of goals and the design of goal-directed machinery was one of the founding principles of AI and its ancestor, cybernetics. Essay 6 contains a short explanation of the General Problem Solver (GPS), an early goal-directed AI architecture. Marvin's psychological theories (SOM/TEM) may be seen as designs for how minds could contain and manage systems of goals: innate drives, learned goals, sub-goals, interpersonal goals, and meta-goals, all interoperating to produce intelligent behavior.

Goals have a special role in the educational context because an important and neglected key to learning a field of knowledge is *internalizing its goals*. For example, students often find it hard to learn math because it's unconnected to their personal lives and goals. Teachers need to communicate not just the facts and techniques of a field of knowledge, but its goal structures as well—what questions the field is trying to answer, and what makes those questions interesting. This is something standard education typically only accomplishes accidentally when it accomplishes it at all. For instance, you can learn lots of facts about biology without learning to understand and share the deep motivations of the scientists who discover them. Good teachers can sometimes transmit the goals of a field, but more often than not this doesn't happen, leading to students who are alienated from school, dutifully memorizing knowledge detached from the motivations that led to its discovery, and with no ability to connect it to their own goals.

An emphasis on goals does not mean exhortation to mindless efforts—rather the opposite:

> One needs to learn not only what works, but also what to do when failure looms. I don't like that tale of *"The Little Engine that Could"* with its helpless injunction to simply repeat *"I think I can, I think I can."* A better motto would be to think *"perhaps it's time to try something else"* because every setback can offer a chance for a new phase of mental development. (Essay 6)

In Marvin's view of intelligence, skillful thinking requires not only having goals but being able to think about and modify them.

Construction from Parts

> The secret is in finding out how much can come from so few kinds of parts.
> —Marvin Minsky (Essay 1)

Minsky details some of his early fascination with the construction sets of his childhood: Tinkertoy, Meccano, and so on. From this came the central insight that simple parts could be used to construct arbitrarily complex structures, and that these structures had properties of their own, independent of the nature of their components. Brains, minds, and computers all share this compositional quality, although with the latter we have the advantage of being able to know exactly what the parts are, how they behave, and how they relate to each other and to the overall properties of the system.

Programming languages are also construction kits, with parts that children can recombine in novel ways. Systems like Logo and Scratch act as procedural Tinkertoys, enabling exploration, modeling, and discovery in a new and dynamic domain.

A computer made out of Tinkertoys can implement the exact same computation as one made out of circuitry—and so we assume a properly constructed computer could implement the same kinds of mental processes as the brain. With systems composed of parts, the important thing is the relationship between them, not the physical substrate they are made of.

The universality and substrate-independence of computation, the equivalence of computation to any effective process, and the equivalence of computation and mental activity are all deep, powerful, and in some cases controversial ideas. In an educational context, we do not expect to settle these questions—but giving children the tools to make models of their own thinking and behavior allows even the very young to engage with these fundamental issues.

Other Minds

Social processes are crucial to developing high-level goals, and Marvin has a number of insightful critiques and proposals in this area. Consider a term he coined: *imprimers*—the people from whom one learns foundational goals and values. These can be parents, teachers, or peers, but in any case they play a key role in learning because the goals they impart serve to focus and drive everything else a mind does.

Marvin's emphasis on the social nature of learning might come as a surprise to those accustomed to the usual emphasis on the mechanisms of individual minds that is the default methodological stance of AI. Certainly the AI of Marvin's period of greatest activity did not pay a great deal of attention to the social embeddedness of learning and intelligence. But Marvin was not one to let the current limits of computation interfere with his forward-looking theories of mind. More recently, the social transmission of goals has resurfaced as the focus of attempts to mitigate the supposed existential risks of AIs by achieving "value alignment."[2]

Networks as Escape
The vision of OLPC was to build not only a computer for all the world's children but also a network that would connect them with each other and with the wider culture. Marvin saw this as an opportunity for the intellectually inclined student—so often neglected and bullied in mainstream school culture—to find remote mentors or peers on the net. This vision has been realized to some extent by the later development of online learning communities,[3] such as the one centered around the Scratch programming environment from the Lifelong Kindergarten Group at the MIT Media Lab (http://scratch.mit.edu).

Multiplicity
> Until you understand something more than one way, you don't really understand it.[4]

> It's also important to know multiple ways to represent things, so that if one method gets stuck, you can switch to another.
>
> —Marvin Minsky (Essay 5)

Individual minds are composed of a multiplicity of different parts that are skilled in different ways of thinking. And because everyone's mix is different, individual learners must necessarily develop their own cognitive styles.

One recurrent theme of Marvin's writing on learning is how wonderful it is to find new, nonstandard ways of solving problems—and how the standard model of education tends to suppress such methodological creativity in favor of teaching a single, supposedly right way to do things. The constructionist model of education upends this approach by giving learners a rich set of combinatorial parts that facilitates exploring a space of possible approaches.[5]

The Centrality of Reflection

> Human Minds think about what they're thinking about. ... I'm convinced that these "self-reflective" processes are the principal ones that people use for *developing new ways to think*.
>
> —Marvin Minsky (Essay 6)

If there is one grand unifying idea to Marvin's techniques for generating insight and his proposals to fix education (and he might have denied that there was), it is the central importance of reflection: thinking about thinking. Everyone necessarily has to think about their own thinking—it's part of being a human being—but most of our ideas about ourselves are not that good and can be improved.

Minsky believed that computers could be a tool for reflection but also that reflexive heuristics could be identified, named, and taught. The role of computers in education is not merely to be a substitute for teachers or libraries but to be a language and toolkit for creating models, and particularly self-reflective models. And the product of the attempts of Minsky and Papert and their many students to realize this vision is not improved math scores but children who can think deeply about processes, systems, and themselves.

Conclusion

Digital technology has revolutionized the world in many ways and is continuing to do so as it evolves. But one of the key insights of the early AI days seems in danger of getting lost—that computational ways of thinking are powerful intellectual tools, not just for building games and websites but for understanding complex systems, especially minds.

Computation, in other words, provides a sophisticated language for modeling, and one that is accessible to the young and naive. The trick is to encourage children to think of themselves as computers, and to think of computers as potentially human. It was obvious to Marvin (and Seymour) that this idea was not merely valid but enormously *generative* of new insights. Unsurprisingly, it ran counter to cultural prejudices, which viewed machinery as inherently antihuman. To call something mechanical, in common usage, carries strong connotations of mindlessness. Marvin fought against this dichotomy all of his life, and devoted most of his career to figuring out how to make mindful machines.

There are many reasons to pursue the dream of artificial intelligence, whether they be scientific, economic, or simply deriving from whatever force causes life and intelligence to try to replicate themselves in new forms. But there is a subtler reason that I think is implicit in these essays, which is that almost all of our preconceived ideas about the mind are severely wrong and broken (including such ancient concepts as willpower, freedom, consciousness, and innate ability), and this limits us and causes us needless suffering. Computational ideas give us a radically new way to see ourselves, and their power as a tool for human self-reflection has barely been touched. Getting these ideas into the hands of more people, especially children and other learners, may be one of the most important things we can do for human progress.

Essays by Marvin Minsky

Essay 1 The Infinite Construction Kit

Adults worry a lot these days. Especially, they worry about how to make other people learn more about computers. They want to make us all "computer-literate." Literacy means both reading and writing, but most books and courses about computers only tell you about writing programs. Worse, they only tell about commands and instructions and programming-language grammar rules. They hardly ever give examples. But real languages are more than words and grammar rules. There's also literature—what people use the language for. No one ever learns a language from being told its grammar rules. We always start with stories about things that interest us.[1]

The trouble is, people often try to explain computers the same way they explain ordinary things—the way they teach arithmetic by making you learn "tables" for adding and multiplying. So they start explaining computers by telling you how to make them add two numbers. Then they tell you how to make the computer add up a lot of numbers. The trouble is, that's boring. For one thing, most of us already hate adding up numbers. Besides, it's not a very interesting story.

You can't blame teachers for trying to make numbers interesting. But—let's face it—numbers by themselves don't have much character. That's why mathematicians like them so much! They find something magical about things that have no interesting qualities at all. That sounds like a paradox. Yet, when you think about it, that's exactly why we can use numbers so many different ways! Why is it that we get the same kind of result when we count different kinds of things—whether we're counting flowers or trees or cars or dinosaurs? Why do we always end up the same—with a number? That's the magic of arithmetic. It wipes away all fine details. It strips things of their character. The qualities of what you count just disappear without a trace.

Programs do the opposite. They make things come to be, where nothing ever was before. Some people find a new experience in this, a feeling of freedom, a power to do anything you want. Not just a lot—but anything. I don't mean like getting what you want by just wishing. I don't mean like having a faster-than-light spaceship, or a time machine. I mean like giving a child enough kindergarten blocks to build a full-sized city without ever running out of them. You still have to decide what to do with the blocks. But there aren't any outside obstacles. The only limits are the ones inside you.

Myself, I first had that experience before I went to school. There weren't any programs yet, but we had toy construction-sets. One was called TinkerToy. To build with TinkerToy you only need two kinds of parts—just *sticks* and *spools*. The *spools* are little wooden wheels. Each has one hole through the middle, and eight holes drilled into the rim. The *sticks* are just round little sticks of various lengths, which you can push into the spool-holes (Figure 1.1a). The sticks have little slits cut in their ends, which make them springy when they're pressed into the holes, so they hold good and tight.

What's strange is that those spools and sticks are enough to make anything. Some spools are drilled with larger holes, so sticks

pushed through them can turn. You can make *towers*, *bridges*, *cars*, and *bulldozers*. *Windmills*. *Giant animals*. You can put wheels on your cars and make bearings for pulleys and gears, to make them do more interesting things. You have to make the gears yourself: just stick eight sticks into a spool. They work, though not too well, and always go click-click-click when they turn.

The sticks are cut into two kinds of lengths. One series of lengths come in the ratios *one*, *two*, *four*, and *eight*. The other lengths are cut so that they fit across the diagonals of squares made from the first series of sticks. Thus, all the lengths are powers of the square root of two—and this means that you can also use the first kind as diagonals for squares made with the second series of sticks. You can use this to build sturdy cross-braced structures (Figure 1.1b).

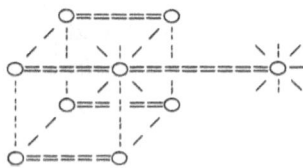

Figure 1.1a

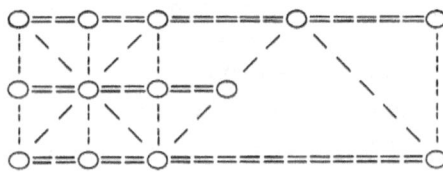

Figure 1.1b

The secret is in finding out how much can come from so few kinds of parts. Once, when still a small child, I got quite a reputation. My family was visiting somewhere and I built a TinkerToy tower in the hotel lobby. I can't recall how high it was, but it must have been very high. To me it was just making triangles and cubes, and putting them together. But the grown-ups were terribly impressed that anyone so small could build anything so big. And I learned something, too—that some adults just didn't understand how you can build whatever you want, so long as you don't run out of sticks and spools. And only just this minute while I'm writing this, I realize what all that meant. Those adults simply weren't spool-stick-literate!

When my friend, Seymour Papert, first invented Logo, I had the same experience again. Logo has some things like sticks—except that their computer commands: a stick 100 units long is called FORWARD 100. Logo also has things like spools: RIGHT 90 starts a second stick at right angles to the last one you drew. I recognized old building-friends at once.

Making Logo programs is a lot like building with construction toys—but it's even better. You can make drawings of things and structures, but you can make procedures, too. You can make them use words. You can make things change their forms. And you can make them interact: just make the properties of some of your objects depend on some features of other objects. As toys, those programs have their faults: you can't take Logo cars outside and roll them down a real hill—but, in exchange, their parts don't get loose and fall out and get lost. And the basic experience is still there: to see how simple things can interact to make more wonderful things.

Logo started many years ago and several writers of this book were children when they helped us find new things to do with it. I'm very pleased to write this essay now, recalling what a great adventure this has been and knowing, too, that it has just begun.

There were other good construction toys, like Erector-Set and Meccano. Erector sets were just great. They had many kinds of parts, but the basic ones were metal strips with many holes, and different kinds of angle brackets. You got a million little screws and nuts to put them together with. They also gave you long, steel shafts, which fit through the holes just large enough to let them turn freely. And there were gears and pulleys to attach to the metal shafts, so you could make complicated things that really work.

The Meccano set, made in England, was even better. It had real brass gears that could more smoothly mesh. When I was older, I built one of the very first modern, remote-controlled robots, using parts of a Number 10 Meccano set, and using ideas invented at MIT's first computer research laboratory in the 1940s. And, speaking of building computers, some of the people in this book[2] once built a real, honest-to-goodness computer out of TinkerToy parts. It could actually compute the moves to play the game called Tic-Tac-Toe. It actually worked, and is now in a museum somewhere. It was made of spools and sticks—and also some string and, since the truth must be told, they hammered in some little brass nails to keep the sticks from falling out. It took about 100 sets, and was too big to fit in your room.

The golden age of construction-sets came to its end in the 1960s. Most newer sets have changed to using gross, shabby, plastic parts, too bulky to make fine machinery. Meccano went out of business. That made me very sad. You can still buy Erector, but insist on the metal versions.[3] Today the most popular construction set seems to be LEGO—a set of little plastic bricks that snap together. LEGO, too, is like Logo—except that you only get

RIGHT 90. It is probably easier for children, at first, but it spans a less interesting universe, and doesn't quite give that sense of being able to build "anything." Another new construction toy is FischerTechnik, which has good strong parts and fasteners. It is so well made that engineers can use it. But because it has so many different kinds of parts, it doesn't quite give you that Logo-like sense of being able to build your own imaginary world.

About the time that building-toys went out of style, so did many other things that clever kids could do. Cars got too hard to take apart—and radios, impossible. No one learned to build much anymore, except to snap-together useless plastic toys. And no one seemed to notice this, since sports and drugs and television-crime came just in time. Perhaps computers can help bring us back.

After you've built something with a "real" construction-set, you have to take it all apart again—or you won't have enough parts for the next project. With programs, you can keep them on your disc and later get them out and build them into bigger ones. This year, you might run out of memory—but that won't be a problem for your future children, because memory will soon be very cheap. What's more, you can share your programs with your friends—and still have them yourself! No emperor of ancient times could even dream of that much wealth. Still, many adults just don't have the right kinds of words to talk about such things—or the kinds of ideas that could help them think of them. They just do not know what to think when little kids converse about "representations" and "simulations" and "recursive procedures." Be tolerant. Adults have enough problems of their own.

To understand what computers are, and what they do, you shouldn't listen to what people say about those "bits" and "bytes" and binary decisions. I don't mean that it isn't true. Computers are indeed mostly made of little two-way switches. But everyone is simply wrong, who says that this is what you need to understand what computers can do. It's just as true that houses can be made from sticks and stones—but that won't tell you much about architecture. It's just as true that animals are mostly made of *hydrogen, carbon, oxygen,* and *nitrogen*—but that won't tell you much about Biology.

> A Martian szneech once mindlinked me; it wanted to know what literature was. I told it how we make sentences by putting words together, and words by putting letters together, and how we put bigger spaces between words so that you can tell where they start and stop. "Aha," it said, "but what about the letters?" I explained that all you need are little dots since, if you have enough of them, you can make anything.
>   The next time, it called to ask what tigers were. I explained that tigers were mostly composed of hydrogen and oxygen. "Aha," it said, "I wondered why they burned so bright." The last time it called, it had to know about computers. I told it all about bits and binary decisions. "Aha," it said, "I understand."

Computer Programs Are Societies

You really need two other facts to understand what computations do. The first idea is that making a big computer program is building a larger process out of smaller ones. I suppose you could truthfully say that sculptors make large shapes from stuck-together grains of clay. But that shows what's wrong with the bits-and-bytes approach. No sculptor ever thinks that way, nor scientist, nor programmer. An architect first thinks of shapes and forms, then walls and floors, and only last about how those will be made.[4]

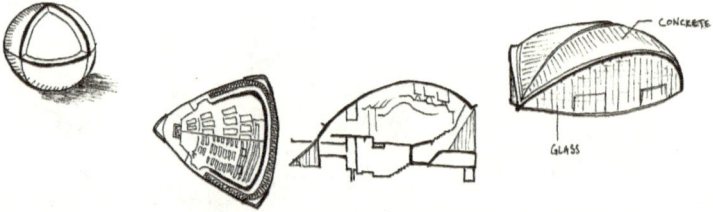

And that's the second important idea that most people don't really understand, but people like Logo users can: it doesn't matter very much what kinds of parts you start with! Even if we start with different kinds of computers, with different kinds of parts inside—still, they mostly can be made to do the same things at the top level. In the same way, you can build a big windmill with either wooden sticks or metal beams. When you look closely, each part will be quite different. But at the top level, both windmills will have a base, a tower, and a propeller. The same is true for computers!

> *Any computer can be programmed to do anything which any other computer can do—or which any other kind of "Society of Processes" can do.*

The Infinite Construction Kit

Most people find this unbelievable. How could it be that what computers do does not depend on how they're made? This was discovered about 50 years ago by an English scientist named Alan Turing. He showed that, just as sculptors needn't care about how grains of clay are shaped, programmers needn't care how all those small computer parts work! For example, Logo programs start with simple "true-false" choices, which depend on one thing at a time. But then we can write a Logo program to choose from a list of things—and we could make that list include a thousand million billion things!

What Alan Turing showed would take too long to explain here and you can find the details in any good book about the theory of computers. But here's the general idea. When Turing was quite young, he realized that what a computer does only depends on the *states* of its parts—and on the laws that change its states. Except for that, it doesn't matter how the parts are made. Turing asked what are programs? He then realized that you could think of programs as just sets of states or, rather, as ways to pre-arrange how a computer will, later, change its States.

Next, Turing thought, suppose you have one computer X but wish that you had a different kind of computer, Y. Then why not make a program for X that re-arranges its States so that, from then on, they will act just like the States of the other computer, Y? If that were done then, from now on, X's behavior will look exactly like Y's—to anyone watching from outside. Today, a

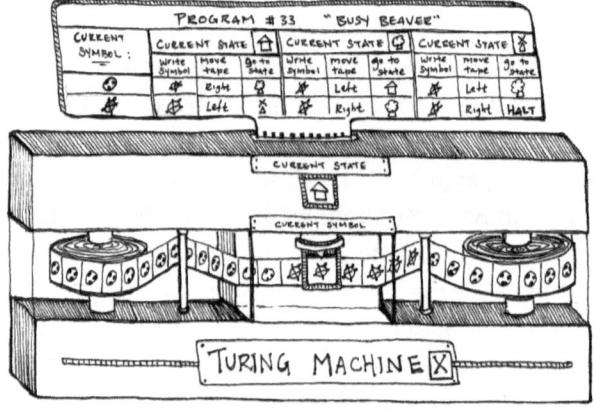

programmer would say that X is "simulating" Y. Of course you have to pay a price for this. It won't work at all unless X has enough memory to hold a description of Y. And if X and Y are very different, then the simulated programs will run very slowly. But aside from that, Turing showed, any kind of computer can be programmed to simulate any other kind! That is why we can write special programs to make the same Logo programs run on all the different computers in the world.

In fact, every Atari Logo system contains just such a program. It was written by Brian Silverman and his friends.[5] I'm sorry that you can't read it. The trouble is, it's not written in Logo but in a machine-language buried deep inside your machine. But it's there, hiding out of sight, making your computer simulate a Logo computer. The strange thing is that Alan Turing figured out how to do such things 50 years ago, in 1936, long before computers were even invented! How could he do that? He simulated them inside his head.

This must be the secret of those magical experiences I had, first with those construction-sets and, later, with languages like Logo. There's something "universal" about the ways that big things don't depend so much on what's inside their little parts.

The Infinite Construction Kit

What matters is more how the parts affect each other—and less about what they are, themselves. That's why it doesn't matter much if money's made of paper or of gold, or houses out of boards or bricks.

Similarly, it probably won't matter much if aliens from outer space had golden bones instead of ones of stones, like ours. People are missing something important, who don't appreciate how simple things can grow into entire worlds. They find it hard to understand Science, because they find it hard to see how all the different things we know could be made of just a few kinds of atoms. They find it hard to understand Evolution because they find it hard to see how different things like birds and bees and bears could come from boring, lifeless chemicals—by testing

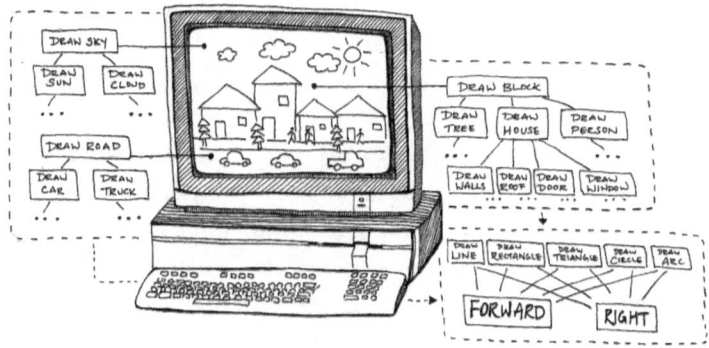

trillions of procedures. The trick, of course, is doing it by many steps, each using procedures which have been debugged already, in the same way, but on smaller scales.

Why don't our teachers tell us that computers have such glorious concerns? Because most adults still believe the only things that computers can do are huge, fast, stupid, but useful calculations of arithmetic. And so those dreary practicalities of billion-dollar industries crowd out our dreams and fantasies of building giant mind-machines.

Marvin Minsky and the Ultimate Tinkertoy

Alan Kay

Let me confess in advance: I love Marvin! I say this in the present tense because only his physical body passed away—Marvin lives on vividly in the minds of all who were fortunate enough to know him, either personally or through his many talks and writings like the ones in this book. I think most people who read these will also come to feel they know him, as "the Marvin of Ideas" starts to live on vividly in their minds. As Mike Travers points out in his excellent introduction to this book, one of Marvin's main rules of thumb is that we should try to internalize great thinkers inside our own minds in such a way that *they can keep thinking to help us think*. I'm going to try to do this—to "channel Marvin"—in this afterword.

I have especially loved this particular essay of Marvin's because he wrote it for child readers to help support a large vision he believed in: that the new medium of computing, if really understood and used well, could make an enormous positive difference in helping children grow up with a much more powerful view of the world and a set of mental tools for dealing with that world. He appeals directly to children because they are the touchers of computers most likely to see what computers are really about, whereas most adults—including many computer professionals—have wound up adopting very weak notions about computing.

> A key difficulty in learning "powerful ideas" is that we always start "where we are," and try to fit new ideas and things into what we already think we know. If the new ideas/things are very different, then we often either bypass them entirely or force them into distorted meanings that fit our current "private universe": the one between our ears! Marvin would like children to always have the thought: "I think this idea/thing is this way, but it could also be another way, and it could be made from things I'm not thinking about at all." (Marvin was great at this rule of thumb!)

Marvin uses analogies to Tinkertoys because there is an amazing range of things that can be made from a few simple parts—very like bricks and other simple fundamental building blocks, and especially like "computer stuff." Marvin was a fabulous Tinkertoy builder as a child and knew, as every child discovers, there is immense satisfaction in building something that turns out *just right*. The learning comes freely from the joy of happily focusing on making something neat. As Maria Montessori pointed out many years ago, play is the work of the child.

The first thing we usually do with Tinkertoys is make structures that go beyond the parts. If we start fooling around with the parts we'll come up with *something*. I wound up with a skyscraper tower (figure 1.2).

We can see right away that what's most important about Tinkertoys is not the details of the components. Other construction materials will have their own basic components and ways to be put together. Most of the powerful ideas are in the designs of the combinations.

Figure 1.2

> A good way to think of this powerful idea is: *As more complex things are made, architecture dominates materials*! In other words, what lies behind what we touch and think about are often wonderful things that are mostly *organizational* in nature. As Marvin says in essay 1, "What matters is more how the parts affect each other—and less about what they are, themselves."

Some of the Tinkertoy parts allow movement, so we can make a toy vehicle that we can push or pull around. Maybe a tractor with a cab?

What about vehicles that are automobiles, that can go by themselves? Tinkertoy does not provide direct ways to make such vehicles, but we can improvise them. For example, we can put the tower we made on our vehicle, make a weight from something heavy (like coins in a baggie), and use our string to wrap around the rear axle to be pulled and turned by the weight.

Figure 1.3

If we look at our self-powered vehicle, we can see that it is not smart enough to prevent itself from crashing into a wall or falling off a table. Could we make it smart enough to avoid these? And what do we mean by "smart"?

Figure 1.4

Marvin worked with Seymour Papert for many years in a joint quest for good working models of intelligence. They started looking beyond traditional programming and computing for better parts, organizations, and designs to make "thinking stuff."

One source of inspiration came from the field of cybernetics, which Marvin had delved into while in college, and another from the autonomous and somewhat intelligent robot tortoises of Grey

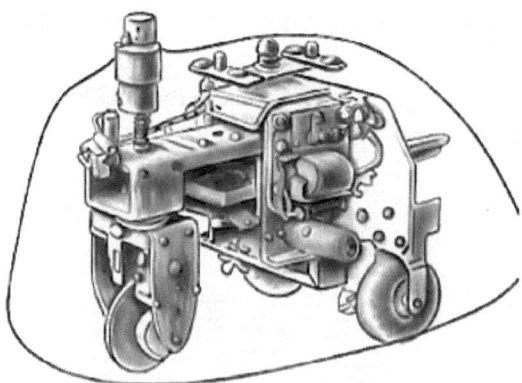

Figure 1.5

Walter, which could not only negotiate arbitrarily complex environments but also learn a conditioned reflex (like Pavlov's dog). Marvin knew Grey Walter, and Grey Walter's ideas helped inspire the later Logo turtle geometry system for children.

Marvin and Seymour could see that most interesting systems were *crossconnected* in ways that allowed parts to be *interdependent* on each other—not hierarchical—and that the parts of the systems needed to be *processes* rather than just "things."

At the same time that he wrote this essay, Marvin was writing a book about how minds might work—called *The Society of Mind*—and said in the beginning: "To explain the mind, we have to show how minds are built of mindless stuff, from parts that are much smaller and simpler than anything we'd consider smart. ... But what could these simpler particles be, the 'agents' that compose our minds?"[1]

We've just made several Tinkertoys that are *more able* than their parts. Can we use Tinkertoys to make *agents* that are *smarter* than the agents that are their parts?

The Infinite Construction Kit

In order to make our self-powered vehicle smarter, we have to make it able to sense what is going on far enough ahead of time to make something happen that will cause the vehicle to stop before any disaster occurs. One way to do this is to give it a "sensor probe" that will make contact with barriers in front of the vehicle and connect the probe to a brake that will activate when the probe touches something. If we extend the probe out the back, then we'll also have a "prod sensor" that will release the brake when our vehicle is bumped from behind and prompt it to start up and move out of the way.

Children are very happy when they have a big idea, build it, and have just enough Tinkertoys parts to make it! But then more parts are still needed because as ideas get built they also cause new and better ideas to appear.

One of the many wonderful things about computers—especially today—is there are always enough parts for any idea, and those ideas definitely cause more wonderful ideas to appear. There is essentially no friction, and no limits these days except for our imaginations.

> What the children are doing with toys like Tinkertoys are *intellectually honest versions of what adults do*—in this case, the designing and building parts of engineering and art. The design process has not been removed from them by giving them prefabbed special parts and pre-done designs by others (as many contemporary "construction toys" do today). Too much pre-purposing puts success, no matter how empty, ahead of the joyous struggles of learning and doing. Real learning of powerful ideas and the power that comes from them are the results of the big changes that happen *in our minds* as we struggle with, eventually grasp, and become fluent with the difficult-to-learn ideas. Many "learning difficulties" are critically important! Seymour Papert called this "Hard fun."[2]

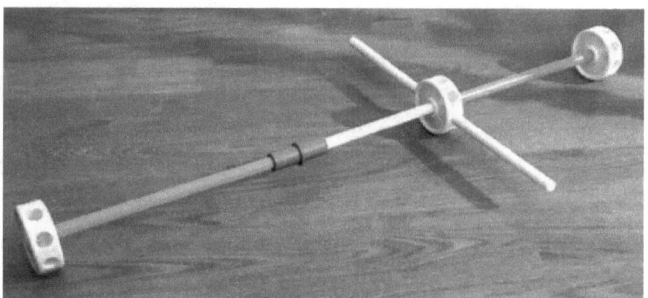

Figure 1.6a

Figure 1.6b

The Infinite Construction Kit

Inspired by Grey Walter's robot tortoises, a brilliant idea for the Logo world was to make a physical turtle for children to program. Its "mind" would be supplied by programs they would write! This brings what Grey Walter so cleverly did with a few wires and vacuum tubes into their world in a real and deep way.

The combination of a physical turtle with a children's programming language brought out the best of both worlds, and many interesting projects were invented, including making the turtle more able by telling it how to draw and do things—and having the children learn real mathematics in the bargain.[3] The project to make the turtle "smarter" by having children build little brains for it to think and learn with let the children gain important insights into biology,

Figure 1.7

psychology, themselves, and *thinking itself* (as Marvin and Patrick Winston discuss insightfully in essay 6 and its introductory remarks).

For example, the following figure shows a simple Logo program—an "agent made from mindless actions"—for getting the turtle to carry out the Grey Walter "explore" behavior. Over and over, the turtle will go forward "a little" and then randomly turn somewhere between 45 degrees to the left and 45 degrees to the right.

```
to wander
  forever
    forward 10
    right (random 90) - 45
```

— "**to**" means define a procedure, with the following name
— "**forever**" means do what is indented below over and over
    Move turtle **forward** 10 little steps
    Turn turtle to the **right** the number of degrees given by doing the arithmetic

Figure 1.8

I'll now turn to a descendent of Logo—a drag-and-drop blocks programming language called GP for *general purpose*; it is easily accessed online through any web browser.[4] GP has several useful and more modern features in addition to what Logo provided. Figure 1.9 shows the same Grey Walter "wander" program done in GP.[5]

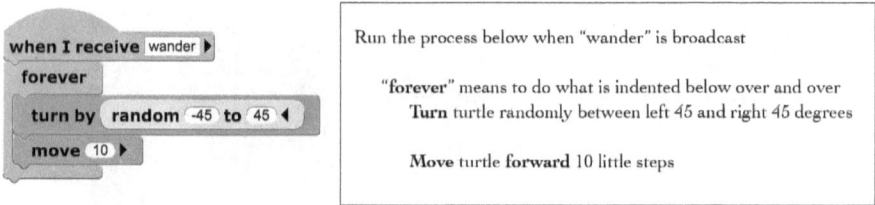

Figure 1.9

This program is more "able" than "smart" because it can be trapped by walls and other obstacles. Let's add in an "avoid"

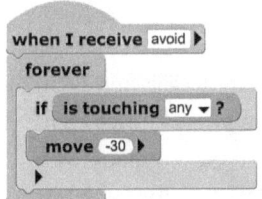

Test to see if we are touching something
    If yes, jump turtle backwards 30 little steps
    If no, just do the forever again

Figure 1.10

behavior to run simultaneously. It will use the touch sensor to see if we've bumped into something, and if so, we'll want to jump back.

Note that there is always a random turn whether going forward or backward, and this helps the turtle eventually get away from an obstacle (figure 1.11). Does the track of the turtle remind you of the much later "Roomba"? Two simple agents can make a lot happen!

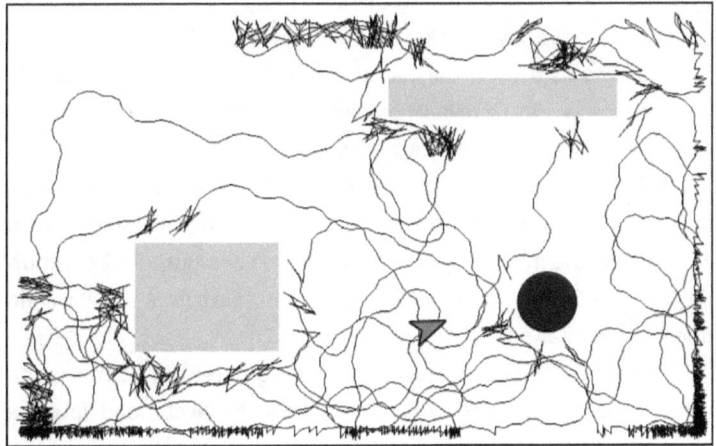

Figure 1.11

Tinkertoy Is the Ultimate Thinkertoy

The "TicTacToe"-playing computers done by Danny Hillis and Brian Silverman, then two of Marvin's students and now well-known computer scientists, almost show the limits of what can be made with Tinkertoys. These computers included many ideas that the inventors of Tinkertoys never thought about!

Tinkertoys' limits here are not logical—it is logically possible to build a whole computer out of them—but practical. Tinkertoys have various kinds of errors, frictions, and other difficulties that add up to a frozen immobility after a point. The second, simpler Tinkertoys computer was created to minimize as many practical difficulties as possible.

We can see why Marvin used Tinkertoys as an analogy in essay 1 for the nature and powers of children to "make things come to be, where nothing ever was before" via designing and programming. We make not just to have, but to *learn*—first with our hands and eyes that can feel and see, and then, by stepping back to think more deeply, we move from "tinkering" to "pondering." Adding the computer allows us to turn our handmade things and ponderings into dynamic behaviors to give us qualitatively more to think about. Not just Tinkertoys—computers are "Thinkertoys"!

In designing and programming on computers, we are following in a long tradition that Marvin had a part in, one that started with Sketchpad, the invention of modern interactive graphical computing by Ivan Sutherland in 1962. Sutherland's advisors were Marvin and Claude Shannon.

We can see today's personal computing here! Just as the rough sketch of a bridge was easily transformed by Sketchpad fifty-five years ago into a dynamic simulation that calculated the stresses and strains as well as showed the appearance of the bridge, today we can have children draw diagrams of animal neural structures, make them work, and try them out in simulated animals. Sketchpad was done on a supercomputer the size of a football field. Today's children have vastly more computer power at their disposal on their personal laptops that cost only a few hundred dollars and are the size of just the Sketchpad display (the football field–sized computer is now on the back of the display, and much faster!).

Figure 1.12
Brian Silverman and Danny Hillis, *TinkerToy TicTacToe Computer*, 1975. Image courtesy of Mid America Science Museum.

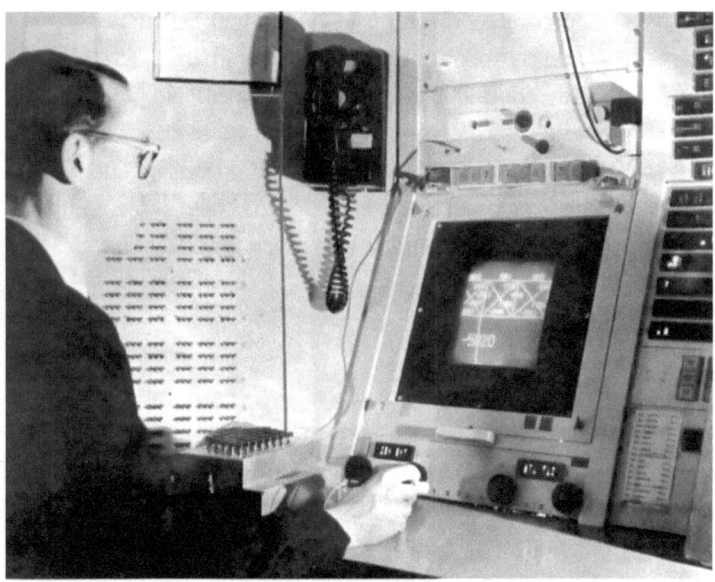

Figure 1.13a
Ivan Sutherland, *Ivan Sutherland Operating the Sketchpad System*, 1963 [digital image]. http://www.dspace.cam.ac.uk/handle/1810/243359. Courtesy of Creative Commons 2.0 License.

Marvin had a part in how laptops and children's computers came about. When I was in grad school at the University of Utah in 1968, Marvin gave an exciting talk at a nearby educational computer conference, and much of it was about Seymour and his thoughts on helping children learn powerful ideas.[6] Later that year I visited Seymour's and Cynthia Solomon's Logo classroom outside of Boston, and what they were doing blew my mind—and still does to this day! On the plane back to Utah, I made this sketch of "a personal computer for children of all ages": a "dynamic medium for creative

The Infinite Construction Kit

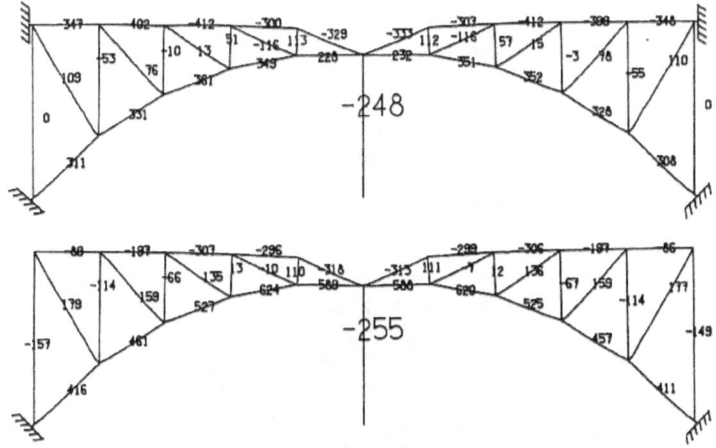

Figure 1.13b
Ivan Sutherland, *Diagram of Bridge Loading Forces Created Using Sutherland's Sketchpad*, 1963 [digital image]. http://www.dspace.cam.ac.uk/handle/1810/243359. Courtesy of Creative Commons 2.0 License.

thought" inspired by Sketchpad, Logo, and other ideas from our research community. This was part of what grew into the personal computers, laptops, and tablets we now use.

The children of 2018, learning about how conditioned reflexes work by programming working models that bring their sketches to life, are using ideas and technologies directly descended from Ivan, Marvin, Seymour, Cynthia, and the other pioneers of that time. The examples in this afterword show that what's really important about computers, especially for children, is how they can go beyond

Figure 1.14

imitating conventional media to give rise to new and dynamic ways to represent ideas, understand and learn complex systems, model scientific theories, and create new art and artifacts that cannot exist without them.

What do *you* think children should be doing with their computers?

Acknowledgments

I am deeply indebted to John Maloney for extensive help in shaping the computer examples in GP and for very helpful critiques of the writing. I'd like to thank Yoshiki Ohshima for valuable insights. Thanks also go to Mike Travers, who pioneered many of the ideas for modeling animal minds for children. And I'd also like to thank K-5 instructional technology teacher Jen Lavalle for a careful critique that increased clarity and understandability. Most of all I want to thank the many dedicated teachers we've worked with over the years—we've learned a lot from you!

Finally, thanks to Cynthia Solomon and Xiao Xiao for inviting me to write this afterword to one of my favorites of Marvin's writings. And it's been great to join my friends and colleagues of many years (many decades!) to celebrate one of our most delightful and influential mentors. It's been a lot of fun putting this together!

Introductory Remarks to Essay 2

Hal Abelson

Reading through Marvin's essay I'm reminded of nothing so much as sitting through one of his lectures: a rapid-fire barrage that left listeners scrambling in an attempt to follow the stream of associations and variations that floated in and out while riffing on a common theme. Marvin had the rare ability to sit down at the keyboard and improvise a Bach-like fugue; his talks were like those fugues.[1]

And so it is with this essay/fugue on math education. Marvin begins with a forthright exposition of the principal theme: learning math should be about inventiveness. That theme is precisely opposed to the common view of math education as teaching kids to follow rules of logical thinking or, worse yet, making kids do arithmetic drill and practice. For Marvin, it's all about inventiveness, not rules. As Codirector of the MIT Artificial Intelligence Laboratory, one of Marvin's maxims about lab policy (rules) was that policies are what you follow when you don't have a better idea. In this vein, this essay on math contrasts a boy who saw math as a never ending succession of rules when faced with the chore of learning the multiplication tables, with a girl who added 15 and 15 by starting with 16 plus 16 is 32 and then removing two 1's. Marvin comments that

Marvin at the piano

a traditional teacher might tell the girl she was wrong to not have followed the rules.

The fugue proceeds from that comment to introduce a variation on the principal theme: that an emphasis on getting an accurate answer might be the wrong thing in teaching arithmetic, and that learning to estimate might be more useful for everyday life, along with allusions to floating-point arithmetic versus fixed-point arithmetic. That variation develops into the more general observation that primary school curriculum as a whole is out of date, given a century of progress in computing.

Marvin's essay/fugue next introduces a countersubject (second theme): students need cognitive maps of their subjects, not only in math but in all of them. This notion of cognitive maps is in line with Seymour Papert's emphasis on "powerful ideas" in Logo, and Andy diSessa's view of learners as epistemologists.[2] After all, to invent one needs a space to invent in and a sense of the intellectual terrain. With these ideas as a springboard, Marvin introduces a flurry of "bringing mathematics to life" questions that could populate a veritable playground of ideas in school mathematics: Why are triangles rigid? Why is prime factorization unique? What insights can we get from game theory? Statistics? Logic? Topology? And more.

The takeaway message here is that school mathematics is impoverished and disempowered because it does not come with a rich enough vocabulary of ideas. As Marvin writes, "*It is hard to think about something until one learns enough terms to express the important ideas in that area*" (essay 2).

As the fugue unfolds, we're treated to the kinds of tangential associative leaps that made listening to Marvin's lectures so delightful: Why do teachers tell students to show their work—wouldn't it be better to improve students' working memories? Doesn't education really require apprenticeship—perhaps we can help kids find mentors through intellectual dating services? Can we study the widespread aversion to math to discover ways to teach about aversion to things? This section ends with a nod at the fugue's opening theme: perhaps we should encourage math students to invent their own new ways to do arithmetic problems rather than repeat the same methods over and over.

Finally, as with proper fugues, there's a coda: AI research (and Marvin in *The Emotion Machine*) has emphasized the importance of learning from negative examples and correcting mistakes. Maybe the emphasis on making learning enjoyable is discounting the value of frustration and negative reinforcement. After all, as Marvin said, "anything worth doing is worth doing badly."

And with that, the piece ends, leaving us admiring, wondering, and wishing for more and more clarification, just like one of Marvin's talks.

Essay 2   What Makes Mathematics Hard to Learn?

Why do some children find Math hard to learn? I suspect that this is often caused by starting with the practice and drill of a bunch of skills called Arithmetic[1]—and instead of promoting inventiveness, we focus on preventing mistakes. I suspect that this negative emphasis leads many children not only to dislike Arithmetic, but also later to become averse to everything else that smells of technology. It might even lead to a long-term distaste for the use of symbolic representations.

> *Anecdote: A parent once asked me to tutor a student who was failing to learn the multiplication table (Table 2.1a). When the child complained that this was a big job, I tried to explain that because of diagonal symmetry, there are less than 50 facts to learn (Table 2.1b).*

	2	3	4	5	6	7	8	9
2	4	6	8	10	12	14	16	18
3	6	9	12	15	18	21	24	27
4	8	12	16	20	24	28	32	36
5	10	15	20	25	30	35	40	45
6	12	18	24	30	36	42	48	54
7	14	21	28	35	42	49	56	63
8	16	24	32	40	48	56	64	72
9	18	27	36	45	54	63	72	81

Table 2.1a

	2	3	4	5	6	7	8	9
2	4	6	8	10	12	14	16	18
3		9	12	15	18	21	24	27
4			16	20	24	28	32	36
5				25	30	35	40	45
6					36	42	48	54
7						49	56	63
8							64	72
9								81

Table 2.1b

However, that child had a larger-scale complaint:

> Last year I had to learn the addition table and it was really boring. This year I have to learn another, harder one, and I figure if I learn it then next year there will be another one and there'll never be any end to this stupid nonsense.

This child imagined 'Math' to be a continuous string of mechanical tasks—an unending prospect of practice and drill. It was hard to convince him that there would not be any more tables in subsequent years.

To deal with the immediate problem, I made a deck of "flash cards," each of which showed two digits on the front and their product on the back. The process was to guess each answer and, if it was correct, then to remove that card from the deck. This made the task seem more like a game in which one can literally *feel* one's progress as the size and weight of the deck diminishes. Shortly the child excitedly said, "This deck is a really smart teaching machine! It remembers which products I've learned, and then only asks for the ones I don't know, so it saves me from wasting a lot of time!"

What Makes Mathematics Hard to Learn?

However, a more serious problem was that this child had no good image or "cognitive map" of what might result from learning this subject. What function might Math serve in later years? What goals and ambitions might it help to achieve?

Anecdote: I asked a certain 6-year-old child "how much is 15 and 15" and she quickly answered, "I think it's 30." I asked how she figured that out so fast and she replied, "Well, everyone knows that 16 and 16 is 32, so then I subtracted the extra two 1's."

> *Traditional teacher: "Your answer is right but your method was wrong: you should add the two 5's to make a 10; then write down the 0 and carry the 1, and then add it to the other two 1's."*

The traditional emphasis on accuracy leads to weakness of ability to make order-of-magnitude estimates—whereas this particular child already knew and could use enough powers of 2 to make approximations that rivaled some adult's abilities. Why should children learn only "fixed-point" arithmetic, when "floating point" thinking is usually better for problems of everyday life!

More generally, we need to develop better ways to answer the questions that kids are afraid to ask, like *"What am I doing here, and why?" "What can I expect to happen next?"* or *"Where and when could I find any use for this?"*

I'll conclude with a perceptive remark from MIT's Phil Sung:[2] *"Students are being led to think that they dislike math when they actually just dislike whatever it is that they're being taught in math classes."*

Students Need Cognitive Maps of Their Subjects

Until the 20th century, mathematics was mainly composed of Arithmetic, Geometry, Algebra, and Calculus. Then the fields of Logic and Topology started to rapidly grow, and in the 1950s we saw a great explosion of new ideas about the nature of information and computation. Today, these new concepts have become so useful and empowering that our math curriculum is out of date by a century. We need to find ways to introduce these ideas into our children's earlier years.

In the traditional curriculum, Arithmetic was seen as so absolutely foundational that all other mathematical thinking

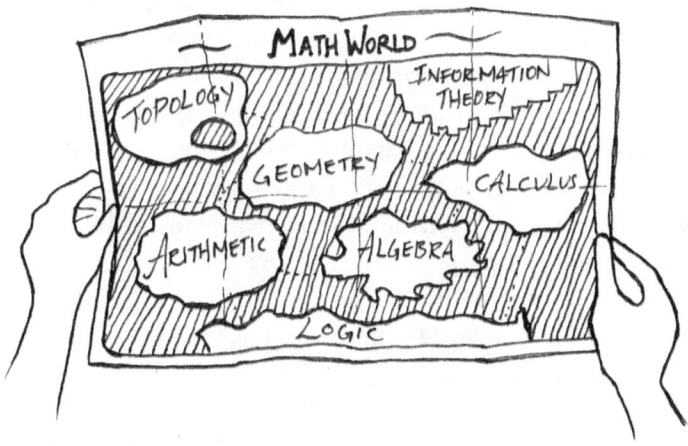

depended on it. Accordingly, we sentenced all our children to two- or three-year terms of hard labor at doing addition, multiplication, and division! However, today it might be better to regard those tasks as little more than particular examples of algorithms—and this suggests that we could start, instead, with some simpler and more interesting ones!

For example, we could engage our children's early minds with simple examples and ideas about Formal Languages and Finite State Machines.[3] This would provide them with thoughtful and interesting ways to think about programs that they could create with the low-cost computers that they possess. Programming languages like Logo and Scratch can help children experiment not only with simple arithmetic, but also with more interesting aspects of geometry, physics, math, and linguistics! What's more, this would also empower them to apply those ideas to develop their own ideas about graphics, games, and languages—which in turn could lead them to contribute practical applications that their communities can develop and share.

Similarly in the realm of Geometry, we can provide young children with interactive graphical programs that can lead them to observe and explore various sorts of symmetries—and thus begin to grasp the higher-level ideas that mathematicians call the "Theory of Groups"—which can be seen as a conceptual basis not only for Arithmetic, but for many aspects of other subjects. (To see examples of such things, type "Geometer's Sketchpad" into Google.)

Similarly in the realm of Physics, children can have access to programs that simulate the dynamics of structures, and thus become familiar with such important concepts as stress and strain, acceleration, momentum, energy—and vibration, damping, and dimensional scaling.

In any case, we need to provide our children with better cognitive maps of the subjects we want them to learn. I asked several grade-school teachers how often they actually used long division. One of them said, "I use it each year to compute the average grade." Another teacher claimed to have used it for filling out tax forms—but couldn't recall a specific example. But none of them seemed to have clear images of mathematics as a potential lifetime activity. Here is a simple but striking example of a case in which a child lacked a cognitive map:

> A child was sent to me for tutoring because of failing a geometry class, and gave this excuse: *"I must have been absent on the day when they explained how to prove a theorem."*

No wonder this child was confused—and seemed both amazed and relieved when I explained that there was no standard way to

What Makes Mathematics Hard to Learn?

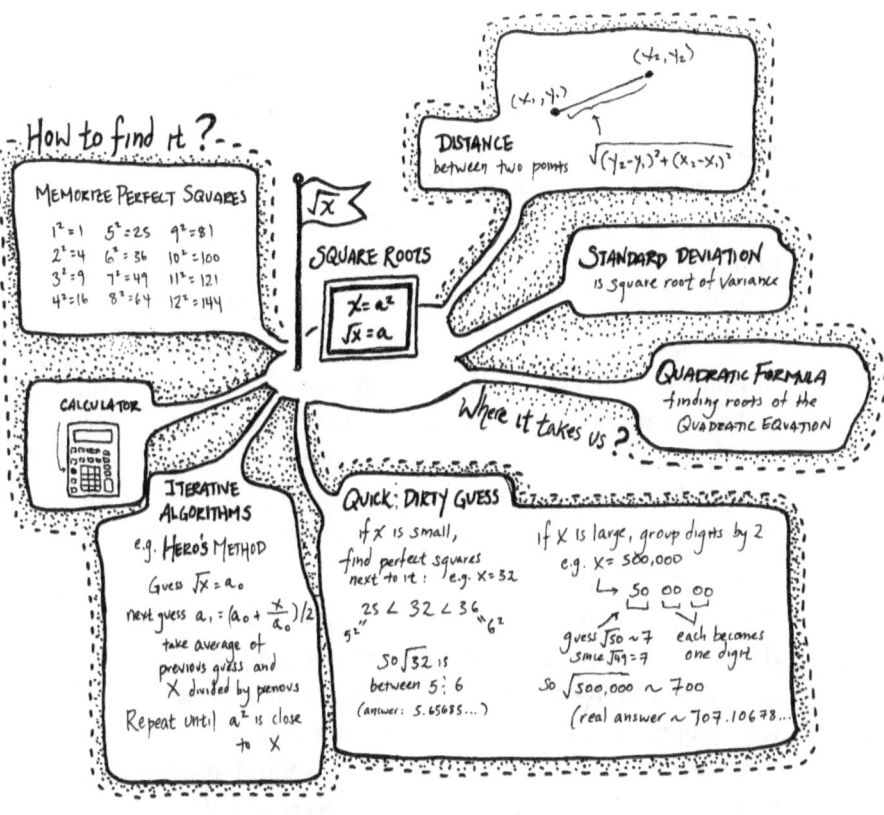

make proofs—and that "you have to figure it out for yourself." One could say that this child simply wasn't told the rules of the game he was asked to play. However, this is a very peculiar case in which the 'rule' is that there are no rules! (In fact, automatic theorem-provers do exist, but I would not recommend their use.)

Bringing Mathematics to Life

What is mathematics, anyway? I once was in a classroom where some children were writing Logo programs. One program was making colored flowers grow on the screen, and someone asked if the program was using mathematics. The child replied, "Oh, mathematics isn't anything special: it's just the smart way to understand things." Here are a few kinds of questions that pupils should ask about the mathematical concepts we ask them to learn:

Arithmetic: Why does "compound interest" tend to add more digits at constant rates? How do populations grow? How does recursion lead to exponentiation? It is easy to understand such things when one experiments with computer programs, but not when a child is constrained to the tedious rate of boring numerical calculation.

Geometry: How many different ways can you paint 6 colors on the faces of a cube? Can you envision how to divide a cube into three identical five-sided objects? We know that gloves come in left- and right-hand forms—but why are there only two such versions of things? We all live in a 3-D world, but few people learn good ways to think about 3-D objects. Shouldn't this be seen as a handicap?

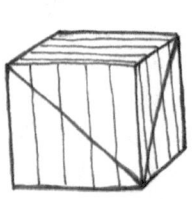
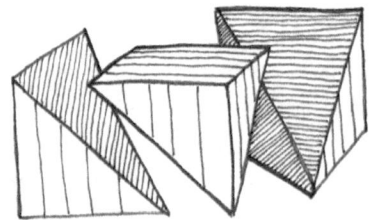

What Makes Mathematics Hard to Learn?

Logic: If most A's are B's, and most B's are C's, does this imply that many A's must also be C's? Many adults will give the wrong answer to this! Is it possible that when John Smith moved from Apple to Microsoft, this raised the average IQ of both companies? We all try to use logical arguments, but we also need to learn about the most common mistakes!

Mechanics: What makes a physical structure stronger when one braces it with triangular struts? That's because two triangles are congruent, when their corresponding sides are equal—which means that there's no way to change a triangle's shape, once the lengths of its sides are constrained. Today most children grow into adults without ever having learned to use the basic concept of "degrees of freedom."

Statistics: Few mathematical subjects rival Statistics in the range of its everyday applications. How do effects accumulate? What kinds of knowledge and experience could help children to make better generalizations? How should one evaluate evidence? What's the difference between correlation and cause? Every child should learn about the most common forms of biases—and also about why one needs to be skeptical of anecdotes.

A very few fragments of knowledge about statistics can illuminate most other subjects. In particular, it seems to me, that we should try to get children to learn to use the "T-test" method, which is an extremely simple statistical test, yet, one that handles huge ranges of situations. (To use it, one only needs to know enough about the powers of 2!) Also they should understand using square roots to assess variations. (You can estimate a square root simply by halving the number of digits!) Example: Basketball scores often turn out to be number pairs like 103 to 97—which are not statistically significant!

Combinatorics: Consider that, when we teach about democracy, few pupils ever recognize that, in an electoral-college voting system, a 26% minority can win an election—and if there are 2 tiers of this, then a mere 7% minority could win! How do cultural memes manage to propagate? How does economics work? At what point should we try to teach at least the simplest aspects of the modern Theory of Games?

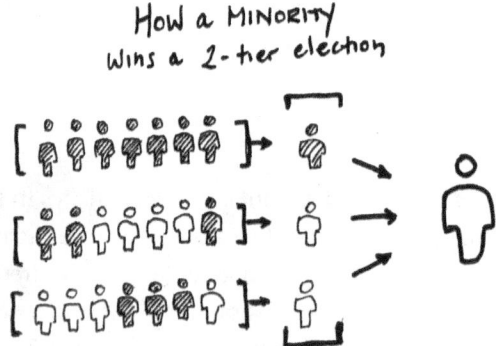

Abstract Algebra and Topology: These are considered to be very advanced, even postgraduate. Yet there are many phenomena that are hard to describe if one lacks access to those ideas—such as fixed-points, symmetries, singularities, and other features of dynamic trajectories, all of which appear in many real-world phenomena. Every large society is a complex organization that can only be well described by using representations at many different levels of abstraction—e.g., in terms of person, family, village, town, city, country, and whole-world economy—and "higher mathematics" has many concepts that could help to better understand such structures.

How can we encourage children to invent and carry out more elaborate processes in their heads? Teachers often insist that pupils "show their work"—which means to make them "write down every step." This is convenient for making grades, as well as for diagnosing mistakes, but I suspect that this focus on 'writing things down' could lead to mental slowness and awkwardness, by discouraging pupils from trying to learn to perform those processes inside their heads—so that they can use mathematical thinking in 'real time.' It isn't merely a matter of speed, but of being able to keep in mind an adequate set of alternative goals and being able to quickly switch among different strategies and representations.

The Impoverished Language of School-Mathematics

There's something peculiar about how we teach math. If you look at each subject in elementary school—History, English, Social Studies, etc.—you'll see that each pupil learns hundreds of new words in every term. You learn the names of many organizations, leaders, and wars; the titles of many books and their authors; and terms for all sorts of ideas and concepts—thousands of new words every year.

However, in the case of school-mathematics, the vocabulary is remarkably small. The children do learn words for various objects and processes—such as *addition, multiplication, fraction, quotient, divisor, rectangle, parallelogram, cylinder, equation, variable, function,* and *graph.* But they learn only a few such terms per year—which means that in the realm of mathematics, our children are mentally starved, by having to live in a "linguistic desert." *It is hard to think about something until one learns enough terms to express the important ideas in that area.*

What Makes Mathematics Hard to Learn?

Specifically, it isn't enough just to learn nouns; one also needs adequate adjectives! What's the word for when you should use addition? It's when a phenomenon is *linear*. What's the word for when you should use multiplication? That's when something is *quadratic* or *bilinear*. How does one describe processes that change suddenly or gradually: one needs terms like *discrete* and *continuous*. To talk about similarities, one needs terms like *isomorphic* and *homotopic*. Our children all need better ways to talk about, not only Arithmetic and Geometry, but also vocabularies for the ideas one needs to think about statistics, logic, and topology. This suggests that communities set up discussion groups that encourage the everyday use of mathematical terms—communities in which a child can say "nonlinear" and have others admire, and not discourage her.

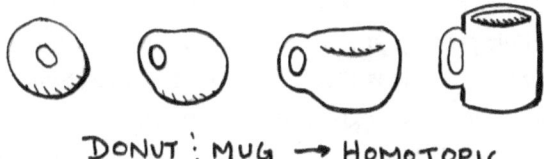

DONUT : MUG → HOMOTOPIC

Mentors and Communities

If one tries to learn a substantial skill without a good conceptual map, one is likely to end up with several collections of scripts and facts, without good ways to know which of them to use, and when—or how—to find good alternatives when what you tried has failed to work. But how can our children acquire such maps? In the times before our modern schools, most young children mainly learned by being forced to work on particular jobs, and ended up without very much 'general' competence. However, there always were children who somehow absorbed their supervisors' knowledge and skills—and there always were people who knew how to teach the children who were apprenticed to them.

I'll come back to this in Essay 3 about the disadvantages of modern age-based classes. Today most education is broader, but apprenticeship itself is rare, because few teachers ever have enough time to interact very much with each of their students: a modern teacher can only do so much. The result is that no one has time to deal thoroughly with questions like *"What am I doing here, and why?" "What can I expect to happen next?"* or *"Where and when am I likely to use this?"*

However, now we can open new networks through which every child can communicate. This means that we can begin to envision, for each of our children, a competent adult with enough "spare time" to serve as a mentor or friend to help them develop their projects and skills. From where will all those new mentors come? Perhaps that problem will solve itself, because our lifespans are rapidly growing. The current rate of increasing longevity today is one more year for every four, so *soon we may have more retired persons than active ones!*

Of course, each child will be especially good at learning particular ways to think—so we'll also need to develop ways to match up good "apprenticeship pairs." In effect we'll need to develop "intellectual dating services" for finding the right persons to emulate!

In any case, no small school or community can teach all possible subjects, or serve the needs of individuals whose abilities are atypical. If a child develops a specialized interest, it is unlikely that any local person can be of much help in developing that child's special talents and abilities. (Nor can any small community offer the range of resources to serve children with limited abilities.) However, with more global connections, it will be easier to reach others with similar interests, so that each child can join (or help form) an interactive community that offers good opportunities.

(Some existing communities will find this hard to accept, because most cultures have evolved to reward those who think about the same subjects in the same ways as do the rest! This will pose difficult problems for children who want to acquire new ways to think and do things that their neighbors and companions don't do—and thus escape or break out of the cultures in which they were born.)

Emphasizing Novelty Rather Than Drudgery?

Actually, I loved arithmetic in school. You had to add up a column of numbers and this was fun because there were so many different ways to do it. You could look here and there and notice three 3's and think, "that's almost a 10 so I'll take a 1 off that 7 and make it a 6 and make that 9 into a 10." But how do you keep from counting some numbers twice? Well, you could think: "Now I won't count any more 3's." How many children did these things exactly as they were told to do? Surely not those who became engineers or mathematicians! For when you use the same procedure again, there's little chance to learn anything new—whereas each new method that you invent will leave you with some new mental skill (—such as a new way to use your memory).

For example, when you add 6 and 7 and write down a 3, how do you remember to "carry" a 1? Sometimes I'd mentally put it on my shoulder. How do you remember a telephone number?

Most people don't have too much trouble with remembering a 'local' 7-digit number, but reach for a pen when there's also an area code. However, you can easily learn to mentally put those three other digits into your pocket—or in your left ear, if you don't have a pocket!

Why are so many people averse to Math? Perhaps this often happens because our usual ways to teach arithmetic insist on using certain rigid skills, while discouraging each child from trying to invent new ways to do those things. Indeed, perhaps we should study this subject when we want to discover ways to teach aversions to things!

Negative Expertise

There is a popular idea that, in order to understand something well, it is best to begin by getting things right—because then you'll never make any mistakes. We tend to think of knowledge in positive terms—and of experts as people who know exactly what to do. But one could argue that *much of an expert's competence stems from having learned to avoid the most common bugs.* How much of what each person learns has this negative character? It would be hard for scientists to measure this, because a person's knowledge about what *not* to do doesn't overtly show in that individual's behavior.

This issue is important because it is possible that our mental accumulations of counterexamples are larger and more powerful than our collections of instances and examples. If so, then it is also possible that people might learn more from negative rather than from positive reinforcement. Many educators have been taught that learning works best when it seems pleasant and enjoyable—but that discounts the value of experiencing frustrations, failures, and disappointments. Besides, many feelings that we regard as positive (such as beauty, humor, pleasure, and decisiveness) may result from the censorship of other ideas, inhibition of competing activities, and the suppression of more ambitious goals (so that, instead of being positive, those feelings actually may reflect the workings of unconscious double negatives). See the longer discussions of this in Sections 1-1 and 9-4 of *The Emotion Machine*.[4,5]

Introductory Remarks to Essay 3

Gary Stager

Although profoundly interested in learning and a gifted teacher, Marvin Minsky gave blessed little attention to K–12 education as an institution. He agreed viscerally with his friend Seymour Papert that schools are bad places for children to learn because they are such bad places for teachers to learn. I suspect that Marvin knew the actual details of day-to-day schooling were worse than he might imagine. None of this means that he called for the destruction of schools or thought little of teachers—quite the contrary. In all of my encounters with Marvin, he was more than respectful of teachers and was interested in their work, thoughts, and aspirations. His comfort with schoolteachers was aided by his inattention to the daily minutia, bureaucratic lunacy, and crackpot pedagogical theories of the world in which teachers operate. Perhaps one can only be a fabulous inventor, scientist, raconteur, pianist, and composer by ignoring the indignities of schooling. But these essays indicate he was indeed aware of various sides of schooling.

Like Papert, Minsky possessed the empathy necessary to recognize that everyone in the world was not like him. At its core, his essay on grade-based segregation is a respectful acknowledgment of diversity.

The longstanding tradition of organizing education by grade-level segregation has its roots in a yearning for a simplistic notion of industrial age efficiency. Its continuing practice may only be viewed as naiveté born of superstition and ideological certainty. The practice defies common sense. Heterogeneous and multiage learning is the norm everywhere outside of school. There are also contemporary examples of effective multiage learning found in schools, not only in multiage primary classrooms but also in instrumental music, choir, drama, and sports. I once heard Papert refer to age-based segregation as grouping kids by similar levels of incompetence.

Mechanistic aspects of schooling, including age-based segregation, subject departmentalization, and the fifty-minute period are rooted in our culture's unwillingness to recognize that learning is natural. Such recognition would result in much more school flexibility and what Seymour Sarason called "productive contexts for learning."[1] As Minsky writes in this essay:

> more generally, children develop at different rates, and each one learns in different ways—so when you put many students in the same room and try to teach the same things to all of them, some will flourish while others get stressed, and some forge ahead while others get lost. Whatever it is that we want to teach, it is hard to design an age-based curriculum that suits the needs of pupils with different abilities.

Students have much to learn with and from not only peers of different ages, but also adults. Jean Piaget teaches us that knowledge is a consequence of experience.[2] Lev Vygotsky, Jean Lave, and Etienne Wenger remind us that much knowledge is socially constructed.[3] Having access to diverse expertise enriches the learning process. One way in which schools may make use of adult expertise is by introducing children to things they don't yet know they love.

For eight consecutive years, Marvin Minsky generously hosted "fireside chats" with the K–12 educators attending my Constructing

Effects of Grade-Based Segregation

Modern Knowledge summer institute. Marvin would spend an hour or two speaking with the educators about any topic. He never disappointed. Each year, one of the greatest scientists of the past century treated classroom teachers like colleagues and shared the full range of his intellect, humor, empathy, mischief, playfulness, and wonder. Each year, I attempted to run the event *and* film Minsky's fireside chats, yet his aura seemingly caused innumerable cameras and recorders to fail. Still, I do remember a number of profound points Marvin made during these events that add to the "Effects of Age-Based Segregation" essay. (These are not verbatim.)

Hobbies Seem to Be a Good Model of Optimum Learning

Although during one fireside chat Marvin argued against joy, fun, religion, sport, and music as frivolous (or worse) pursuits, he did express an admiration for the sorts of learning that emerge through hobbies. Hobbies feature continuous increases in complexity, may be social or solitary, and engage multiple skills and disciplines. I suspect that Marvin would have shared Seymour Papert's notion that the richest learning emerges when a person is engaged in "hard fun."[4] Hobbies do not abide by the strictures of the school calendar or grade levels.

Problem Solving

One educator asked, "Marvin, what do you do when confronting a really hard problem?" Marvin thought for a moment and said, "Don't worry about the problem. Find the right person." Then in the world's greatest humble brag, Minsky continued, "I never worried about solving a difficult problem. I always knew I could call Robert Oppenheimer, John von Neumann, or Claude Shannon." Later in the conversation, Marvin was asked a question along the lines of, "What should we do about schools?" He paused briefly and wistfully replied, "I never worried about those sorts of questions. I knew I could always just ask Seymour [Papert]."

School Structure as a Curricular Impediment

Marvin once told our group that a major problem plaguing education is that there is no structure allowing for the teaching and learning of topics that may only require ten days to learn. School days are divided into short periods and the academic calendar is divided into semesters, trimesters, or marking periods. The result is that students miss out on experiencing powerful ideas that could be learned in a matter of a couple weeks. Marvin offered information theory as such a domain.

Learning by Making

Although considered the father of artificial intelligence and a computer science pioneer, I understand that Marvin did not enjoy programming, at least in comparison to inventing things, playing the piano, or tinkering. While I do not have research to support this intuition, I suspect that accomplished people share a formative experience of learning with their hands. A ninety-nine-year-old Jerome Bruner told me that building and racing boats on the Hudson as a boy was critical to his intellectual development. Seymour Papert had his gears. Marvin told us that it was a shame that today's kids don't have access to junkyards like his generation did. He expressed a belief that the leaders of post-war science benefited from access to abundant military surplus "junk" as children.

Marvin Minsky supercharged any classroom, lab, or living room into the greatest context for learning. He was interested in anything anyone else found interesting, even if only to wonder why you had such an interest or belief. Having known him just a little bit is one of the highlights of my life. Sharing his genius and spirit with educators brought me indescribable joy. Although he was never my teacher, I will continue to learn from Marvin for the rest of my days.

Essay 3 Effects of Grade-Based Segregation

Most large schools assign same-aged children into groups, where they're all taught the same curriculum. We justify this system of "grades" by claiming that it helps to prevent inequities in size and strength, or that it promotes efficient teaching because those children will tend to have similar capabilities. It also is argued that that system helps with "socialization"—a process in which the pupils learn and share similar outlooks, opinions, and values. Surely this process should help them to improve their mutual understanding (if only to the extent to which it gets them to think in more similar ways).

However, a different view of this suggests that age-based segregation might actually retard our children's development:

> *A new class of 6-year-old children will soon begin to share similar ways to think and behave. Then, next year, when they are 7 years old, most of those pupils will still remain in that group—and thus will tend to perpetuate those same patterns of activity. The next year, they will be 8-year-olds, but will continue to share many attitudes, values, and cognitive strategies. So as those children proceed through their K–12 grades, large portions of their ways to think will remain much like those of 6-year-olds!*

Here's an example that shows this persistence of infantile attitudes: consider that a typical graduate of our schools can recount great numbers of anecdotes about hundreds of actors, athletes, fashion models, and other so-called 'celebrities'—whereas very few of our modern adults can name even a single philosopher, scientist, or scholar. Our age-based system of education does not appear to instill our kids with the qualities that we profess to admire. (Essay 4 will talk more about the importance of how children select their models and mentors.)

> *Citizen: You seem intent to sacrifice the carefree years of childhood, and to fill them instead only with ways to advance their intellectual development. But intelligence is not the only thing that makes our lives worth living: what about love and companionship? Surely it is important for children to have friends who share many common interests.*

Effects of Grade-Based Segregation

Of course, the classroom is not the whole of life: children can also learn from older acquaintances, including their parents, teachers, and other mentors. And we certainly don't want to see young minds being hurt by too much competitive anxiety. Still, we should be concerned that excessive attachment to same-age companions could hamper a child's developing better ways to think about both social and mental activities—and I don't know of any good evidence that age-graded classes contribute much to healthy social relationships.

As for those "carefree" aspects of childhood, we need to examine what might be involved when children engage in what we call "play." Adults often assume implicitly that there is a basic opposition in which Work is seen as 'serious' (and often coupled with discomfort and pain), whereas Play is seen as 'frivolous' (and mainly connected to pleasure and fun). But when we look more closely at Play, we see that it often involves extreme degrees of focus, intensity, and discovery—so much that many of us might recognize, in retrospect, that never since our childhoods have we ever made ourselves Work so hard!

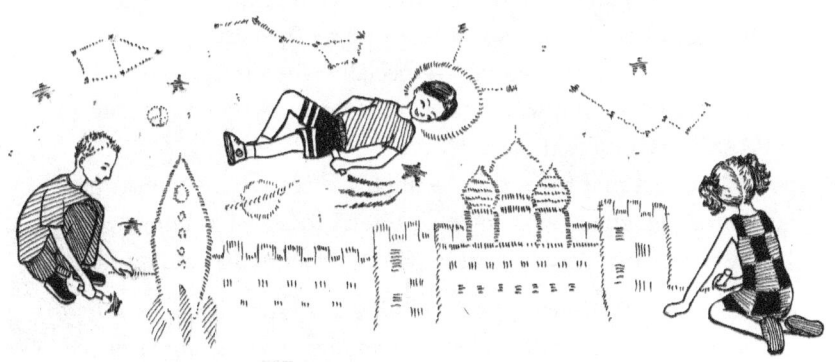

The 50-Minute Hour

Another problem with classroom-based schooling is that it requires a synchronized schedule: each activity must be constrained to some prearranged 'period' of time, after which each child is forced to switch to some different subject or topic. This may be efficient for management, but surely is not the most effective way to develop each child's abilities—or those of the people who teach them.

Those time-limited periods are sometimes justified by assuming that most children have short "attention spans," but I don't see any sound basis for this. Indeed when unlimited time is available, children sometimes show degrees of persistence that rival those of adult professionals—especially when pursuing what we call "hobbies." But when does a child get the time to pursue an idea for as long as it needs?

I suspect that there may be important variations in how people manage their "working memories." To see what I mean, contrast these two descriptions of how a person works out an idea:

Student 1: Whenever I get a good idea, I need to work on it right away—because, if anything interrupts my thoughts, that new concept may quickly fade away. So, most of my accomplishments have come from setting everything else aside, to work on my latest new idea for several hours immediately after conceiving it. Accordingly, when attending a lecture, I always try to sit close to an exit—so that if the speaker says something interesting, I can escape to contemplate it.

Student 2: I don't much mind interruptions because I'm always multitasking anyway. In fact, I don't like thinking about anything for more than about a minute or two, but I don't mind switching a lot between ideas because I don't have trouble with getting back.

I can't recall any research on this, but surely someone has studied it. In any case, I have the impression that some people can develop ideas during many separate intervals—whereas others require longer, unbroken spans of time. If so, then we need to make (and test) theories about what could account for differences in their abilities to *recreate a previous mental process or state* after an interruption or change of subject.

This might also relate to the extent to which different people can take and use notes. Some teachers insist that their students take notes—and even require pupils to hand them in for grading.

> *Student 1: I learn a lot from taking notes, because otherwise I can't remember much from a lecture. However, just writing a few words from time to time is enough to help me reconstruct a lot of what was talked about.*

> *Student 2: I can scarcely take notes at all because it is such a strain to condense what the teacher just said that I miss everything he said after that. In fact if I keep taking notes, then later I can barely remember the lecture at all!*

Here again, we see individual differences; some students can postpone reflective thinking by taking notes, but this doesn't work well for others because their notes don't help them enough to reconstruct the relevant mental processes.

I'm sure that children vary greatly in their abilities to recreate previous mental states, and surely this has a huge effect on how those different children learn because it will affect how they make their Credit-Assignments. I don't have room to explain

Effects of Grade-Based Segregation

this here, so look at Section 8-5 of *The Emotion Machine*.[1] The essential point of efficient learning is that, after you have solved a problem, it is not enough just to remember the answer: you need to remember the strategies that you used to discover that answer. Allen Newell pointed this out in his seminal paper on how to make a smart chess-playing machine.

> Allen Newell 1955: "It is extremely doubtful whether there is enough information in "win, lose or draw," when referred to the whole play of the game [so, for learning to be effective], each play of the game must yield much more information. ... If a goal is achieved, its subgoals are reinforced; if not they are inhibited. ... Every tactic that is created provides information about the success or failure of tactic search rules; every opponent's action provides information about success or failure of likelihood inferences and so on."

I should note that we still don't have learning programs that work this way, perhaps because most research on learning machines has emphasized statistical inference rather than reasoning. In any case, all this suggests that clock-based classes would not be good for those who can't tolerate interruptions.

Children Have Different Cognitive Styles

There is no such thing as a "typical child" because each individual person's brain contains many different kinds of resources—and when different combinations of these are active, this can result in many different "Ways to Think." Thus each child develops different ways to represent various kinds of knowledge and skills—so for a particular child, there will be some situations or activities at which that child might become more (or less) competent than some other children would. But because we don't know very much about how all those resources are organized, we tend to use vague words like "think" and "learn" for many kinds of processes. (See Chapters 7 and 9 of *The Emotion Machine* for more ideas about those processes.) In any case, each roomful of children will contain ones who tend to learn in different ways:

Effects of Grade-Based Segregation

- Some children do well by beginning with abstractions and "top-down" descriptions.
- Others prefer to start with examples, and then to generalize them.
- Some do better with brief intervals of study; others do better when they can spend hours.
- Some learn best from verbal descriptions; others gain more from graphical pictures.
- Others learn best from reading texts, while others prefer to listen to lectures.
- Yet others learn more from manual and tactile interactions with physical materials.
- Some children prosper with many easy problems; others thrive on fewer but harder ones.
- Perhaps some children learn more from success, while others learn more from their failures. I don't know of any hard evidence for this; however among mathematicians it's widely agreed that one learns less from seeing examples of things than from studying counterexamples of things.

Most children have individual interests—hobbies, pastimes, and even obsessions—which may not be seen by their teachers as unrelated to the standard curriculum. Yet each person will eventually need to find some profession or job in society—and while most people do find useful roles, quite a few end up with nothing to do, and this can be tragic or dangerous. This suggests that we should take care not to classify a child's "peculiar special interest" as being an eccentricity that interferes with that child's "normal" progression toward a "general education." Instead, in many instances, it might be better to recognize and encourage those individualistic preoccupations.

More generally, children develop at different rates, and each one learns in different ways—so when you put many students in the same room and try to teach the same things to all of them, some will flourish while others get stressed, and some forge ahead while others get lost. Whatever it is that we want to teach, it is hard to design an age-based curriculum that suits the needs of pupils with different abilities.

In older times, this problem was recognized—and many pupils were "skipped" a full year or two whenever this seemed appropriate. A famous mathematician I know attributes much of his success to being skipped from Grade 3 to Grade 8. Today this is politically unpopular, but in larger schools, "advanced placement" is still permissible—but only for a particular subject, not for an entire school year.

Socialization

It is often assumed that interacting with other children helps social development more than associating with adults. But it might well

Effects of Grade-Based Segregation

be quite the other way around. In any case, any method of raising children will have consequences on the children's eventual development, and this includes decisions about how we influence our children's selections of other children or adults as friends. For whatever one does, it will have an effect, and inaction does not avoid one's responsibility for the outcome. The trouble is we still know so little about how children develop that we can't see what we are responsible for. In particular, we need to know a great deal more about how age differences in friendship influence children's intellectual and social development—and especially about the extent to which this involves various kinds of tradeoffs. (This paragraph paraphrases some remarks by Curt Adams.)[3]

In any case, this discussion is incomplete. What are plausible alternatives to age-based classes? How should such a project like OLPC relate to existing public, private, and home-based schools? Where do Montessori ideas fit in? What kinds of projects are best accomplished by individuals, pairs, or larger groups? What other issues are involved with linking younger and older pupils? For example, how can we exploit the fact that many high-school aged "computer hackers" know more than their teachers do about computers and programming? We still have many more questions than answers.

Introductory Remarks to Essay 4

Brian Silverman

British entertainer Stephen Fry has a great theory about *Star Trek*. He believes that Kirk is caught between Apollonian Spock (who is rational, logical, ordered, controlled) and the Dionysian McCoy (who is emotional, instinctive, passionate). Similarly, on the surface, Marvin's writing sounds very logical and ordered. You just have to scratch that surface, however, to see Marvin talking about emotion and passion. He discusses thinking about feeling as a complement to thinking about thinking.

Here are some quotes taken from across the decades in which Marvin addresses parts of thinking about thinking that lean away from the purely rational and logical.

Seymour Loved Those Gears

In essay 1, "The Infinite Construction Kit," Marvin says, "You can't blame teachers for trying to make numbers interesting. But—let's face it—numbers by themselves don't have much character. That's why mathematicians like them so much! They find something magical about things that have no interesting qualities at all."

It's a challenge to explain how to see the magic in something with no interesting qualities at all. This challenge is at the core of math education and is one that both Marvin and Seymour Papert stepped up to. In the introduction to *Mindstorms*, Seymour talks about a similar kind of magic in his relationship with gears: "I remember that there was feeling, love, as well as understanding in my relationship with gears."[1]

Seymour speculated that a way of sharing the magic was to encourage kids to build personally meaningful artifacts—to build interesting projects out of things that may have few interesting properties. He invented Logo to try to capture this. Marvin was part of the development of Logo from the beginning, adding motion, music, and magic to the system during its early years.

Who Would Its Mother Be?

Many years ago I asked Marvin the following question: "If we built a truly functional AI, who would its mother be?" He answered by saying that I should look up attachment figures in his book *The Society of Mind*.

In "Learning from Role Models, Mentors, and Imprimers," he elaborates on the notion of attachment figures by talking about mentors and imprimers: "When you meet someone whose work you admire, you might want to acquire their skills—but in the case of an imprimer, you may also want to acquire their values, and more generally, to want to become more like that person!"

For Marvin, an important part of intelligence is having a reasonable model for yourself. That model has to come from somewhere. He suggests that it comes in part from people we want to emulate, to imitate, people who exhibit values that we want to share. Marvin says he even occasionally had conversations with the internalized copies of his imprimers. He did admit, however, that those

Learning from Role Models, Mentors, and Imprimers

internalized copies were rarely able to tell him something that he didn't already know.

How wonderful for Marvin to have defined the notion of imprimer when he acted as one for so many of us!

Earth, Air, Fire, Water

In "Music, Mind, and Meaning," Marvin says, "The old distinctions among emotion, reason, and aesthetics are like the earth, air, and fire of an ancient alchemy. We will need much better concepts than these for a working psychic chemistry."[2] I think this is at the core of some of his thinking in his book *The Emotion Machine*. It even starts to explain how you can put the word *emotion* together with the word *machine*. They don't seem to have a lot of overlap, but that could simply be a consequence of the old alchemy. Reason, aesthetics, and emotion are all products of the same society of mind.[3] The difference is that the agents that deal with emotions never operate close enough to the surface for us to really see how they do what they do.

When reading these essays look not only for Marvin's advice on thinking about thinking but for his advice on thinking about feeling, and also on magic and passion.

Essay 4 Learning from Role Models, Mentors, and Imprimers

> You can't think about thinking without thinking about thinking about something.
>
> —Seymour Papert

Many children dislike the subject called Math because they don't find significant links between those classroom ideas and their everyday lives—so they're left with scattered fragments of knowledge.[1] We all know what frequently happens then: because we failed to provide them with adequate "cognitive maps," many students end up envisioning "Math" as an endless progression of unpleasant tasks.

Now let's take a larger-scale view of what we want our schools to do. Of course we want them to teach the contents of subjects—but we also want schools to "socialize" children—by fostering such civil skills as cooperation and courtesy. And we also ask schools to infuse our children with morals and ethical values, along with suitable goals and ambitions. All this amounts to a very large order—but it seems to me that something important still is missing: *teaching children good ways to think about thinking.* After all, thinking is the principal tool we use to accomplish everything we do.

Accordingly, our schools should try to help their pupils get ideas about how their thinking works and I'm sure that good teachers already do this. However, I'm not proposing to add a Psychology course to the elementary curriculum, because there's no consensus among psychologists about how to augment our mental resourcefulness. So I'll propose a different approach: develop ways to get children to think of themselves as though they were programmed computers!

You might see this as a dreadful idea: how it could possibly help to think of oneself as being like an unfeeling machine. But consider the alternative views that our popular cultures tell us to use:

> *"Each individual is born endowed with certain talents and aptitudes, and those are 'gifts' that we can't give back or exchange—so education can only help us to make the most of what we happened to get.*

Our best ideas come from processes called Intuition and Inspiration, which are magical things that can't be explained—and examining them can damage them."

Such views might seem harmless, but I think they're pernicious: they imply that our minds can't do much by themselves, but can only make selections among the ideas that happen to "come to us."

You might argue that the idea of being a kind of machine should cause even worse feelings of helplessness. However, I'm not suggesting that you should envisage yourself as some kind of unchangeable object—such as a toaster or sewing machine. Instead, I'm suggesting that *if you think of yourself as a thing you can program,* all those constraints will suddenly weaken! For example, when you recognize that you have a "bug," you can imagine that your trouble is caused by some steps in the programs you call your mind. And now, instead of feeling powerless, you can imagine things to find and repair—inside some particular parts of your mind. Of course, this doesn't mean that a person can actually do such things—but this viewpoint could

serve as an antidote to the older belief that we each have a fixed set of "aptitudes," or an unchangeable dose of "intelligence."[2]

Thinking about Thinking about Ways to Think

Suppose you get stuck at achieving some goal. This could lead you to conclude that you're simply not suited for that kind of job—perhaps because you lack certain "talents" or "aptitudes." However, if you can learn to recognize *the particular way in which you got stuck, or the particular kind of trouble you're in*, that diagnosis can suggest more appropriate ways to think. Here are a few examples of these from Chapter 7 of *The Emotion Machine*.[3]

> **If a problem seems familiar,** try reasoning by Analogy.[4] If you solved a similar problem in the past, and can adapt to the differences, you may be able to re-use that solution.
> **If the problem still seems too hard,** divide it into several parts. Every difference you recognize may suggest a separate subproblem to solve.
> **If it seems unfamiliar,** change how you're describing it. Find a different description that highlights more relevant information.

If you get too many ideas, then focus on a more specific example—but if you don't get enough ideas, make the description more general.
If a problem is too complex, make a simpler version of it. Solving a simpler instance may suggest how to solve the original problem.
Reflection. Asking what makes a problem seem hard may suggest another approach—or a better way to spend your time.
Impersonation. When your ideas seem inadequate, remember someone more expert at this, and imagine what that person would do.
Resignation. Whenever you find yourself totally stuck, stop whatever you're doing now and let the rest of your mind find alternatives.
Knowing How. The best way to solve a problem is to already know how to solve it—if you can manage to retrieve that knowledge.
If none of these methods work, you can ask another person for help.

Do we really need to teach such things, in view of the fact that all normal people (including children) already use all or most of these methods? Yes, because, unless we have names for them (or other ways to refer to them) it will be too hard to think about them (so that we can think about improving them). So our conjecture is that many children could greatly augment their resourcefulness if we could provide them with more effective ways to think about their mental processes. (I don't know of any good evidence for this—but that could be because no one has done such experiments.)

Now let's look at possible applications. Every person has some weaknesses that could be seen as "disabilities." For example, some persons are relatively inept at dealing with 3-D spatial relationships, but once we recognize such a deficiency, we can suggest alternative ways to envision things (provided that we can make adequate theories of what might be wrong with the data-structures that person is using). A child once complained to me that she couldn't see how to draw a perspective cube—when I showed her how to draw the appropriate lines, she objected "That looks like a cube but it must be wrong, because cubes don't have any slanted edges." However, this discomfort was relieved when we pointed out that a picture need not correctly represent *all* the features of what it portrays and, often, the essence of making good drawings is finding the right kinds of simplifications. In other words, this child had simply become too ambitious!

Similarly, some children have trouble with memorization—and psychologists know many different "mnemonic" techniques.[5] However, we don't know nearly enough about which techniques could help which children. But we probably could make good suggestions if we guess which kinds of "store" and "load" procedures each particular child tries to apply to the data-structures she's trying to use.

Likewise, many youngsters appear to be deficient in physical dexterity and coordination—and in some cases when physical training doesn't help, this might happen because those children have incorrect mental models of how their bodies work. Then again, if we could diagnose those kinds of "bugs," we might be able to teach those children to improve their "body-images" by using mental, rather than physical training.[6]

It also might even be possible to improve the ways that a person makes higher-level decisions. For example, one can imagine computer programs that could help a person to learn to avoid the common mistakes described in Dan Ariely's *Predictably Irrational* book.[7] Similarly, many people are prone to logical fallacies—and we might be able to develop game-like programs that help young children to acquire better kinds of reasoning.

How Do Children Acquire Self-Images?

> I believe that the obsessive worship of movie, TV and sports figures is less likely to produce spiritual gain than praying to Thor.
> —Chuck Lorre

Some readers may object that intervening to teach about Thinking could be too intrusive (and possibly harmful). Indeed, one might argue that, instead, we should protect young children from such concerns and let them enjoy their carefree childhoods. However, whether we try to guide them or not, our children will still develop ideas about themselves—and the less we influence those self-images, the more they will get them from somewhere else. So now let's explore some questions about how children acquire their ideas about themselves.

We each construct representations of our abilities, goals, aversions, and tastes—as well as of our dispositions, talents, and traits—and of our physical appearances and of our present and future social roles. We often use the term "self-images" for these descriptions of our own characteristics. Of course, we all would like to understand how our brains embody these structures, but no one has yet discovered much about how our brains construct those representations. Section 9-1 of *The Emotion Machine*[8] makes some suggestions about what neuroscientists could try to find in those networks.

From where do our children's self-images come? Of course, they copy a lot from their parents, siblings, teachers, and friends but (as noted in Essay 3) they also tend to emulate familiar public "celebrities," so that many children come to know a lot about athletes, pop-stars, and actors, but few can recognize the name of a single philosopher, scientist, or mathematician, because such achievers are rarely mentioned either in classrooms or media. The images of those celebrities must have substantial effects on our children's goals—yet those descriptions are mainly fictitious, crafted by publicists to grip our children's attention for countless thousands of valuable hours. And even when those biographies are accurate, they don't often demonstrate qualities that we want our children to admire.

For example, consider the extent to which athletic prowess depends on speed and strength—which mainly come from inherited genes. Of course, sports also entail clever strategies—but even in the mental realm, the sport-stories in the media tend to emphasize injunctions like *Try Harder, Don't Quit,* and *Use Guts and Grit*—which emphasize raw doggedness instead of skill and resourcefulness.[9] Similarly, entertainment-scripts tend to glorify leading-role characters whose successes stem from using deceptions or exploiting attractive appearances. More generally, our popular cultures tend to venerate warriors over intellectuals, and rarely depict productive careers. The trouble is that some values acquired in childhood can remain in our minds for the rest of our lives.

We often assess a school's qualities in terms of how many of its students go on to get college degrees. But what of the "dropouts" who depart from that track? We tend to attribute those "academic failures" to deficiencies in persistence, talent, or self-esteem—or to lack of "scholastic aptitude," or to not having enough "intelligence." However, I suspect that it often might be more productive to attribute the trouble to the self-models those children have built. For consider how hard it would be for young children, by themselves, to invent good ideas about themselves; instead, it is far more convenient for them to absorb such ideas from other people they happen to meet. Therefore, we need to be concerned about which of those acquaintances will most influence our children's ambitions, goals, and future roles—because those are the persons who, by default, will be the main sources of those children's self-images.

How Do Children Acquire Their Goals and Ambitions?

You're almost always pursuing goals. Whenever you're hungry, you try to find food. When you sense danger, you strive to escape. When you've been wronged, you may wish for revenge. Sometimes you're aiming to finish some work—or perhaps seeking ways to escape from it. We have a host of different verbs for desiring, such as *try, strive, wish, want, aim,* and *seek*—but we rarely ask ourselves questions about why some goals seem strong and others weak, what decides which goals should be active when, what processes govern how long they'll persist, what happens when several ambitions conflict, and what makes some goals get "too strong to resist"?

(As for what goals are and how they work, I like the explanations offered by Allen Newell and Herbert A. Simon in the early1960s. See the summaries of those ideas in Sections 2-2 and 6-3 of *The Emotion Machine*.)

Learning from Role Models, Mentors, and Imprimers

How do people acquire their goals? Most 20th century theories of learning assumed that each animal begins with certain "basic instincts" that determine what that animal "wants." Later, that animal may learn to connect new sub-goals to those instinctive ones, using processes through which those connections get "reinforced" by rewarding success. Some educational schemes have been based on those theories, but I don't see this as a sound approach, because those old ideas about learning were mainly based on the behaviors of pigeons, dogs, and rats—whereas it seems clear that humans evolved additional levels that go far beyond the "reactive" thinking of animals.

For examples of those higher levels, consider that you often "deliberate" before you react, by first envisioning some alternatives, and going on to evaluate them. Furthermore, you frequently think "reflectively" about your previous mental activities. Finally, you may even go on to "self-conscious reflection" about whether what you have done (or are about to do) is in harmony with what you call your morals, values, or ideals; this level considers not just what one wants, but also what a person *ought* to want. So clearly, those simple, reward-based theories of how most animals learn do not equip us for the task of educating human beings, whose minds have all those additional levels.

In any case, we need to learn more about how each person develops their values and goals. To what extent does this happen by chance or result from making deliberate choices? How much of our children's desires and beliefs are shaped by their inherited genes, and how much by the cultural memes that pervade that child's community? Section 2-3 of *The Emotion Machine* conjectures that we mainly acquire our values from the persons to whom we become "attached." Long ago, an outstanding psychologist recognized this:

> Now since shame is a mental picture of disgrace, in which we shrink from the disgrace itself and not from its consequences, and we only care what opinion is held of us because of the people who form that opinion, it follows that the people before whom we feel shame are those whose opinion of us matters to us. Such persons are: those who admire us, those whom we admire, those by whom we wish to be admired, those with whom we are competing, and whose opinion of us we respect.—Aristotle, in *Nicomachean Ethics*, Book VIII

This suggests that our high-level values are formed in ways that depend on the feelings of pride and shame that come when we receive praise or blame from certain persons. But strangely, we have no conventional name for those particular acquaintances—so we need to introduce a new word!

Imprimer. *An Imprimer is one of those persons to whom a child has become attached.* For animals that raise their young, the function of infant attachment seems clear: remaining close to parents helps to nourish, teach, and protect their offspring. However in humans, attachment has another effect—on the children's ultimate values and goals; when your Imprimer praises you, you feel a special thrill of pride that elevates the goal of your present activity to have some kind of higher priority. Similarly, a sense of shame depresses your present goal's desirability.

When you meet someone whose work you admire, you might want to acquire their skills—but in the case of an imprimer, you may also want to acquire their values, and more generally, to want to become more like that person! It seems clear that our children's values and goals are greatly influenced by those of their imprimers—who are likely to include some of their parents and teachers, as well as some of their classmates and friends. Also, of course, their values and goals may be affected by their encounters with other people—and even by the fictitious heroes and villains they read about. And because all these may influence which kinds of ideas each child will like, our thinking about education must be especially concerned with the attachments our children will make.

What kinds of reasoning do children use to answer the questions they ask themselves? How do they classify the situations they face, and which ways to think will they use in each? What kinds of evidence will they accept or reject, and what will they see as succeeding or failing? We often hear suggestions that children should play a large role in deciding what they should learn—and of course, it will be hard to teach any subject that they have no interest in. However, few children will have enough knowledge to make good decisions about such things, so we look to teachers to provide such help, but the economics of typical schools leaves almost all teachers with too much to do. As for the child's parents and friends, few of them will have the required skills—so most children will need other mentors.

Dictionary entries for "mentor" mention these kinds of qualities: "A trusted counselor who provides advice and support to, and watches over and fosters the progress of, a younger, less experienced person. Someone you trust, respect, and admire—and has a direct interest in your development." Again, a very large order—and we can add to it more: a good mentor must also be a Tutor, to teach the factual content of a field—and should also be a Coach, to train up the needed set of skills—and also should be a Role-Model who can inspire a good set of values and goals.

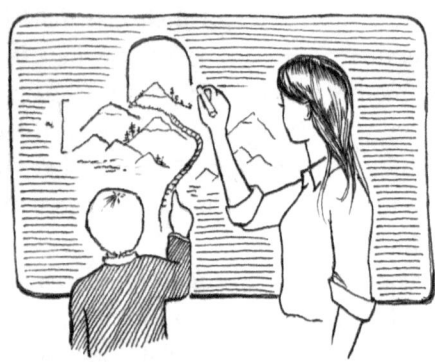

However, perhaps most important of all is for a mentor to teach the postponement of pleasure—that is, paradoxically, to enable you to enjoy the discomforts that come during any significant exploration. Also, good mentors should not just reward you, but should help you find ways to learn from your failures, because on one's expertise comes learning "what not to do"—that is, from learning to know (and then to avoid) the most common hundreds or thousands of bugs! See the discussion of Negative Expertise in *The Emotion Machine*.[10]

Perhaps the most valuable assets of a culture are its potential specialists—so we should put high priority on helping children pursue their interests. When I was a child, adults often said "you shouldn't be so serious" or "take it easy and relax" instead of encouraging commitment and intensity. Such injunctions

Learning from Role Models, Mentors, and Imprimers 95

sometimes also come from other children—and in the microcultures of many schools, well-focused children get called "geeks" or "nerds"—and become the targets of bullies. (Some of those nerds become scornful of "regular" or "normal" kids—and see them as victims of a disorder that might be called "insufficient obsessiveness.") All these are problems our schools should face—but also are ones for which networks can offer escapes.

Finding Mentors in Network Communities

Of course we want to improve our schools, but each teacher can only do so much. However, our new interactive networks offer new ways to freely connect young people to other kinds of mentors and friends, who can offer new opportunities to enter new kinds of communities.[11] Furthermore such networks could help many children escape into more mature cultures and environments—options with special value to children who would otherwise be confined to grow up in noxious local neighborhoods.

This is also important because no small school can teach all possible subjects, or serve the needs of individuals who have atypical abilities. If a child in a small community develops some specialized interest, that child is unlikely to find any local help. The same applies to children with unusual disabilities; no small community can afford the range of resources available to the worldwide network. But as we develop more global connections, it will become more possible to find others with similar interests, and all sorts of specialized services.

Today, our networks are rapidly growing while, at the same time, the world-population is rapidly aging—and this could be a huge new source for mentoring. Soon we'll have hundreds of millions of retired (and child-free) persons, and this will include great numbers of wise and experienced ones who've been left with more than enough "spare time" to mentor great numbers of children. Essay 3 discusses some problems that come from having mainly same-age friends—whereas huge networks of people of varying age will enable young students to interact (and even become apprenticed to) older persons with wider experience.

How can we make productive connections to those millions of faraway mentors? This already happens spontaneously in many thousands of special-interest groups that exist on the World Wide Web. One trouble is that a good many such groups have had cycles in which they flourish, and then deteriorate—so we need to find ways to stabilize them. Perhaps we can get some ideas about this from the websites that succeed at helping consumers with shopping and dating: could we modify that software to make systems that help children to shop for appropriate mentors?

Of course, such suggestions will raise concerns about protecting kids from predators. Clearly, some such problems exist—and many sites already try to prevent adults from joining juvenile groups. However, too much emphasis on safety would reject too many potential mentors, so we should be concerned about the cost-ineffectiveness of hyper-excessive protectiveness.

Introductory Remarks to Essay 5

Walter Bender

Marvin Minsky's theories of mind are largely theories of learning. The central theme of this essay is questioning "general" education with a discussion of "cognitive towers" (levels of mental activity), a construct from the theories laid out in *The Emotion Machine*.[1] These theories encompass both machine learning and people learning and inform one another. Minsky's contributions to "learning by people" are best exemplified by his close collaboration with Seymour Papert and Cynthia Solomon. Minsky had an influential role in their efforts to use the Logo programming language as a vehicle for introducing children to computational thinking, which they define in terms of things to think with and to reflect on.

In 1971, Papert and Solomon published "20 Things to Do with a Computer," a catalog of engaging open-ended projects to explore using Logo.[2] Minsky contributed to many of the "20 things"; his contributions, ranging from robotics to music to the visual arts, directly reflect some of the personal interests that drove his own learning. Throughout the 1970s and 1980s, children used Logo as a tool for the autonomous construction of meaningful artifacts and for solving problems that were personally meaningful.

The "20 Things to Do with a Computer" memo was a harbinger of what is now referred to as the "maker movement," a largely extracurricular collection of activities that offer an outlet for students stifled by trends in general education, which has become increasingly regimented in an era of high-stakes testing and accountability. Arguably, one difference between the maker movement and the work of Minsky, Papert, and Solomon is that *makers* tend to focus on the artifact being created, whereas Minsky and his colleagues focused on the learning associated with the construction of the artifact.

The potential impact of computational thinking on learning was made concrete in Minsky's collaborations with Papert and Solomon, but it has only recently—in the form of programming—evoked interest in mainstream educators. Learning to program is being touted as the cure-all for much of what is allegedly wrong with education: "Even humanities graduates can learn how to code in a few months and join the high-paying digital economy."[3] Through promotions such as "the Hour of Code," programming is being adopted into formal and informal school curricula throughout both the developed and developing world.[4] Although efforts to promote programming are not all superficial, even under the best of circumstances, learning to program in and of itself does not help children "to learn to develop their own, independent ideas." Further, programming at most schools is taught like other "'basic' subjects" as the accumulation of "scattered fragments of knowledge" (essay 5, "Questioning General Education").

The approach to learning to code developed by Minsky, Papert, and Solomon immersed children in problem-solving and debugging. Children were given agency to work on problems they were passionate about in a context in which there was an expectation that there were no predetermined solutions or prescribed paths to a solution. It was in the early 1970s that Solomon first talked about debugging being the greatest learning opportunity of the twentieth century. While engaged in problem-solving, children were developing and refining the algorithms employed by the agents in the various levels of their cognitive towers.

Some of the ideas Minsky expounded are now being realized on a large scale. For example, Finland has questioned general education. Pasi Sahlberg, when discussing the decision to eliminate subject-based classes from the curriculum in Finnish schools, observed that

> integration of subjects and a holistic approach to teaching and learning are not new in Finland. Since the 1980s, Finnish schools have experimented with this approach and it has been part of the culture of teaching in many Finnish schools since then. This new reform will bring more changes to Finnish middle-school subject teachers who have traditionally worked more on their own subjects than together with their peers in school.[5]

Students will be applying tools across disciplines in a manner that better reflects learning across and between multiple mental levels. It will be interesting to observe the impact of this change on generations of Finnish children in the coming decades.

Much has changed since Minsky wrote this essay. It predates the proliferation of smartphones and "apps," Chromebooks and Google Docs, massive open online courses (MOOCs) and online reference resources such as the Khan Academy videos. Educational technology (Edtech) has become big business: selling apps and content is more lucrative and facile than the hard work of engaging teachers and learners in authentic problem-solving. In Edtech, there is a strong temptation to make things as simple as possible so as to reach the broadest possible audience. But some things are inherently complex, and though apps might be fun, the hard part of "hard fun" is in reaching toward that complexity.[6] Children should not miss out on the *playful learning* that takes place while they are learning to use tools to solve real-world problems. The potential for computational thinking and theories of mind to have a positive impact on general education has never been greater.

Essay 5 Questioning General Education

> It is better to solve one problem five different ways, than to solve five different problems in one way.
> —George Pólya

Some parents want their schools to prepare their children for future jobs and careers. Other parents want schools to teach specific sets of ideals and beliefs. Some parents even want their young to learn to develop their own, independent ideas. But regardless of those different goals, most schools assign most of their pupils' time to learning scattered fragments of knowledge about some so-called "basic" subjects—like reading, writing, arithmetic, science, and tidbits of cultural history—and then consume the rest of those children's time with incessant tests and homework assignments.

Surely, that kind of "broad education" helps many children to comprehend many aspects of the worlds they're in. However, I question how well it prepares them to deal with more complex real-world problems—*because it is hard to exploit separate fragments of knowledge until one acquires the mental skills that one needs for retrieving and using the relevant ones.*

Nevertheless, although we rarely teach children about how minds work, quite a few of them do become experts—in what we call their amusements and hobbies—as when they play computer games, or refine their athletic skills, or build structures with construction sets.

> ... the "playfulness" of childhood is the most demanding teacher that one could have; it makes us explore our world to see what's there, to try to explain what all those structures are, and to imagine what else could possibly be. Exploring, explaining and learning must be among a child's most obstinate drives—and never again in those children's lives will anything push them to work so hard.*

Indeed, some children focus so much on their hobbies that their parents fear that this will conflict with their education—and try to find ways to discourage them. However, this essay will propose, instead, to postpone "broad" education until each child has had some experience at becoming an expert in some specialty.

* Section 2-6 of *The Emotion Machine*.

We'll propose to re-aim our schools toward encouraging children to pursue more focused hobbies and specialties—to provide them with more time for (and earlier experience with) developing more powerful sets of mental skills, which they later can extend to more academic activities. These issues are important because our children today are growing up in increasingly complex and dangerous worlds—while our institutions are failing to teach correspondingly better ways to think. The result has been a global pandemic of adults who lack effective ways to deal with increasingly challenging situations.

A Theory of Human Self-Critical Thinking

The Emotion Machine starts with the idea that every brain contains many "resources," some of which recognize various patterns, and others can supervise various actions; yet other resources form goals or plans, and some contain large bodies of knowledge.[1] Then we envision a mind as composed of a multi-level "cognitive tower," whose lowest levels are mainly assembled genetically—whereas the higher-level processes grow in ways that depend less on inherited genes, and more on their interactions with the activities in the levels below them.

Self-Conscious Reflection → Values, Censors, Ideals, Taboos
Self-Reflective Thinking → Constructing Self-Models
Reflective Thinking → Planning and Self-Criticism
Deliberative Thinking → Reason, Search, Compare, etc.
Learned Reactions → Representing One's Experience
Instinctive Reactions → Instinctive Urges and Drives

The Emotion Machine suggests that building such towers is the source of the unique resourcefulness that distinguishes us from other animals. If so, this suggests that a child's first such constructions will have a large effect on the quality of that child's later development.

> *Conjecture: once a child builds a cognitive tower that works well in some particular realm, that child will thereafter be better equipped to develop proficiencies that can be used in other domains.*

The idea is that it seems plausible that the first few such developments could have a major effect on the qualities of that child's future ones—because those will be the child's first experiments with organizing such "vertical" structures. If so, then this would imply that our children's early education should focus on activities, hobbies, and specialties that have the "desirable" kinds of

such qualities. Of course, this also implies that we'll need good theories for which such qualities would be desirable and curriculums that could help to promote them.

In particular, Section 7-5 of *The Emotion Machine* suggests that, at each of those multiple cognitive levels, certain important resources called *Critics* observe some events in the levels below them—and react by selecting which sets of resources would be useful to activate next.

This reorganizes the person's mind to use a different "way to think," of the sorts we mentioned in Essay 4. For example, whenever some mental process gets stuck, one Critic could suggest a way to split the problem into smaller parts (Figure 5.1). Another Critic might recollect how a similar problem was solved in the past. And yet another Critic might suggest a different way to represent the situation.

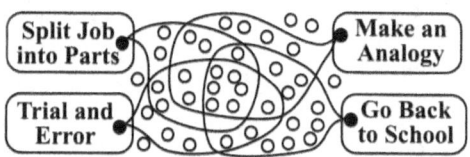

Figure 5.1

If a problem seems familiar, try reasoning by analogy.
If it seems unfamiliar, change your way to represent it.
If a problem seems too hard, divide it into smaller parts.
If it still seems too hard, try a simpler version of it, etc.

What happens when several such Critics are aroused at once? This won't cause much conflict if each of those Critics arouses a different set of resources because, in such a case, a person can "think several ways at once." For example, most of us simultaneously entertain processes involved with social, linguistic, visual, logical, and other kinds of mental processes—e.g., all of the kinds of thinking described in Howard Gardner's view of the mind.

But what if your Critics' suggestions conflict? When multiple Critics try to control some of the same mental resources, then you're likely to "get confused." (What happens when you try to think of two tunes at once?)[2]

If you can't find some compromise, our theory suggests that this condition itself should turn on a higher-level Critic that can detect this particular kind of confusion, and suggest an appropriate remedy. Then, of course, the quality of your hierarchy of Critics will be a major influence on your competence and resourcefulness—especially if, when you're confused, your Critics can diagnose why you're confused.

Abilities, Talents, and Mental Resources

Suppose you get stuck at achieving some goal. This could lead you to conclude that you're simply not suited for that kind of job—perhaps because you lack the right kinds of "talents," or just don't have enough "intelligence." However, if you can recognize *how* you got stuck, this may suggest more constructive alternatives: perhaps you did not activate the right kinds of resources—or need to acquire some new ones, etc.

> Seymour Papert: "Most children seem to have and extensively use an elaborate classification of mental abilities: 'he's a brain,' 'he's a retard,' 'he's dumb,' 'I'm not mathematically-minded.' The disastrous consequence is the habit of reacting to failure by classifying the problem as too hard, or oneself as not having the required aptitude, rather than by diagnosing the specific deficiency of knowledge or skill."

What makes some folks more inventive than others? Why do some outshine others at solving hard problems? Why do some people get stuck less often? The most popular answers to questions like these assume that each person possesses a different amount of some faculty called "Intelligence." However, this doesn't answer those questions at all. It only diverts our attention from them because "intelligence" is one of those suitcase-like words that we use at different times, for different kinds of purposes. We can switch those meanings so fluently that we're rarely aware of doing this. However, as Papert pointed out, once you come to envision yourself as a host of different programs or processes, then, when you disappoint yourself, you can look for ways to "debug" some of those processes!

Select Appropriate Representations: To think about any subject or question, you first need some ways to represent situations, goals, plans, ideas, and relationships—for example, as a verbal description, a pictorial diagram, or a list of constraints to be satisfied.[‡] How can we help our children to learn to develop new, better ways to represent knowledge along with the kinds of processes one needs to manipulate those representations?

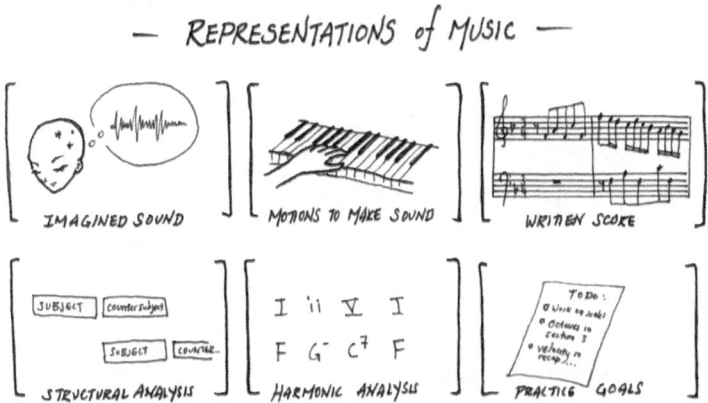

Find Appropriate Analogies: Of course, one of the best ways to solve a problem is to already know how to solve it. However, no two situations are ever exactly the same, so you can't expect to remember an answer—*unless you have also developed processes that can recognize useful analogies.*

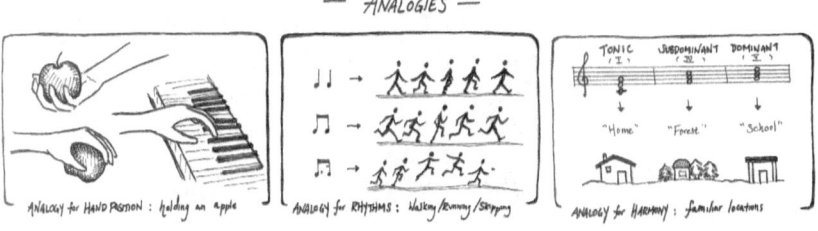

[‡] See Section 8-7 of *The Emotion Machine*.

Negative Expertise: To deal with any hard kind of problem, a person must know some possibly useful strategies—but also one will need to know the most common mistakes that one's likely to make. A superficial survey won't help because one cannot achieve much competence unless, along with each separate fragment of knowledge, one also knows enough about the reputation of that fragment's source, its common exceptions, the contexts it works in, and (when it fails) some alternative paths.

Construct More Realistic Self-Models: Perhaps the most powerful way to solve a problem is to ask, *"What makes this problem seem so hard me?"* But you won't be able to answer that unless you already have good answers to questions like: *How do I make my decisions, and why? How did I get into this situation? What are my goals, and how did I get them? How do I generate new ideas?*

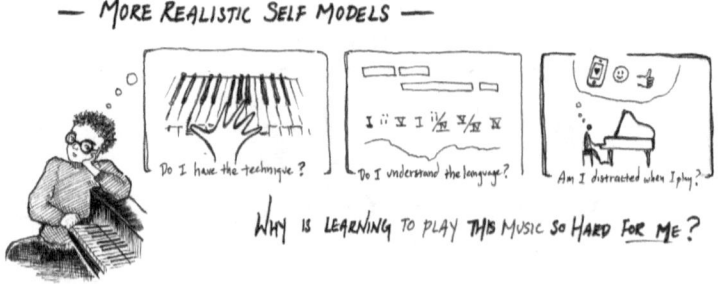

In other words, before you can think about trying to change yourself, you'll need to construct some models of how your mental processes work. However, as Freud recognized a century ago, most of those processes work in ways that can't be directly observed by resources in other parts of your mind; indeed, the higher levels of our mind may even develop ways to suppress or censor such attempts! Nevertheless, by collecting and analyzing evidence, we still can manage to achieve useful levels of self-reflection.

Chapter 7 of *The Emotion Machine* suggests a variety of mental skills that might contribute to our resourcefulness—such as learning that most 'facts' have exceptions, learning the most common kinds of mistakes, avoiding the most common ways to get stuck, and learning what to do when goals conflict. It's also important to know multiple ways to represent things, so that if one method gets stuck, you can switch to another. And perhaps most important of all is the art of making "cognitive maps" of what one learns, so that one can make good decisions about which levels to work on, and when.

Horizontal vs. Vertical Specialties

Some hobbies are conceptually "flat" in the sense that they keep applying similar processes to collections of "same-level" knowledge. We see this when children accumulate objects like comic books or statistical facts about movies or sports. In contrast, other more "vertical" hobbies lead to higher towers of concepts about (for example) the causes, sources, and implications of their lower-level fragments of knowledge—and surely that greater range of mental processes will help one to deal with more challenging situations and problems. Consider some examples of these.

Thinking about Mathematic Concepts: Instead of the conventional trek through the desert of grade-school arithmetic, we can encourage children to start climbing the hills of ideas about symmetries, maps, and analogies—beginning with easy concepts about geometry, logic, group-theory, and topology. Such explorations can lead to more knowledge and power with less effort and time—and eventually make many other subjects easier.

Composing Music or Stories or Plays: Writing stories, sonatas, or songs can involve many levels of plans and designs: one needs to construct a plausible plot and populate it with themes or characters with interesting conflicts and tensions, all of which must be resolved in a structure that one must compress into a single temporal line![§]

[§] See Edgar Allan Poe's "The Philosophy of Composition," www.eapoe.org/works/essays/philcomp.htm. Pictures can tell stories, too—but the two dimensions make it harder to constrain the observer's attention.

Athletics: Competitive, team-based sports are often claimed to help children develop useful ideas about cooperation, tactics, and management skills—and for many children today, this may be their only such activity. However, the enforcement of certain sports in schools causes great fear and shame to quite a few children. To be sure, sports can contribute to physical fitness—but surely we can find alternatives that do not cause so many injuries and disabilities! Also, we ignore the extent to which athletic prowess is largely genetic—hence it's foolish to choose those champions as role models.** Besides, competitive sports don't always promote good social values; instead, they may even encourage wars, by teaching ways to deal with problems by using superior physical force.

Physical Fabrication Crafts: To build a working model airplane, one needs to learn substantial bodies of knowledge, such as the properties of different materials, ways to form and modify them, and ways to combine them into more complex forms. Then eventually, one may come to see why the forces involved require the wing to be stronger near the body than the tips, etc. Consider how many aspects such a project can have: How to shape materials by using knife, saw, file, and chisel—and when and how to maintain those tools? When and how to melt, mold, press, or bend? How to fasten things together by using nails, screws, solders, or glues? How to increase a structure's strength, by making it more rigid or more flexible, or adding additional braces and struts, and stronger adhesives? How do axles and bearing work? What are good ways to store enough energy? How can one minimize friction? More generally, how to plan an overall design?

** See "Running Biomechanics: Shorter Heels, Better Economy," http://jeb.biologists.org/cgi/content/abstract/211/20/3266.

Simulated Fabrications: In recent times, Carpentry has nearly disappeared, and Electronics has turned into opaque "chips"—while Erector and Meccano sets have been replaced by boxes of modular LEGO blocks. However, today, children can simulate physical systems on their computers; for example, with programs like Armadillo Run—or work with tens or hundreds of thousands of rectangular blocks at virtually no fiscal cost (see https://www.lego.com/en-us/ldd/download). Furthermore, today one can email one's mechanical designs to companies that use "3-D Printers" to convert them into working physical models. Such facilities are quite expensive today, but will soon be cheaper (see en.wikipedia.org/wiki/Fab_lab).

Computational Fabrications: Although we may regret the decline of handicrafts, computer programming offers unlimited opportunities to build, test, and apply towers of increasing levels of representations. Hear Seymour Papert describing some early examples of this:

An example of such an experience is writing simple heuristic programs that play games of strategy or try to outguess a child playing tag with a computer controlled "turtle." ... A related example is writing teaching programs—like traditional CAI programs, but conceived, written, developed, and even tested (on other children) by the children themselves. It is said that the best way to learn something is to teach it—and perhaps writing a teaching program is better still in its insistence on forcing one to consider all possible misunderstandings and mistakes. [Similarly, some such] children become passionately involved in writing programs to teach arithmetic and in the pros and cons of criticisms of one another's programs.††

Some Predicaments "Brainy" Children Face

We need to recognize and remedy the common forms of hostility that "intellectual" children are likely to face from popular "jocks" in their communities; they often get called by derisive names like "nerd," "brain," or "geek"—and are often excluded from other cliques. They may even get physical bullying—whereas there is far less such prejudice against children who excel in less technical fields. I suspect that this type of intolerance is a major problem in many schools, and it could have dangerous results: *million*, *billion*, and *trillion* sound much alike, and unless you comprehend such magnitudes, *trillion-dollar deficit* does not sound any scarier.‡‡

---

†† In *Teaching Children Thinking, 1971*, https://dspace.mit.edu/handle/1721.1/5835#files-area.

‡‡ This paragraph is adapted from a message by Christopher Becker.

> Gerald Sussman: My idea is to present an image to children that it is good to be intellectual, and not to care about the peer pressures to be anti-intellectual. I want every child to turn into a nerd—where that means someone who prefers studying and learning to competing for social dominance, which can unfortunately cause the downward spiral into social rejection.

How Can We Help Self-Critical Thinking Develop?

This essay suggests that schools should provide the children with ample time for each to develop some specialties. I'm not proposing to eliminate *all* conventional classroom work, but only to allocate more time to higher-level projects and hobbies, and spend less time on drills, tests, and homework.

Of course, few teachers will have enough time or expertise to supervise so many specialized projects—so those children will need additional mentors—most of whom will have to come from outside. This was impractical in the past—but now we're approaching an era in which a billion retired persons could fill those roles—if we can find ways to connect with them; for every hobby or specialty, we should be able to recruit specialists to give advice and to suggest other ways to proceed.

To what extent can a child's mind spontaneously "self-organize" its higher levels, without any external guidance? To what extent can we help children to learn how and when to make higher-level abstractions or to resort to self-reflection? I've never seen much discussion of this; instead, we assume that such developments happen spontaneously if we just expose a child to the proper kind of curriculum, that a child's mind will somehow construct appropriate systems of processes to represent those experiences. Then, when we come to recognize that some children excel at doing such things, we simply assume that those children are "brighter" than the rest—instead of trying to find out what's happening.

Would it help for us to discuss such things more explicitly? Essay 6 will suggest some ways to include more ideas about minds into our systems for early education.

Introductory Remarks to Essay 6

Patrick Henry Winston

Schools allocate time for learning all sorts of skills, ensuring that children learn how to read, write, calculate, and perhaps name all the state capitals. But what about allocating time for learning about thinking? What would children do during that hour? How could you go a step beyond, teaching them not only better ways of thinking but how to teach themselves better ways of thinking? These are the questions Minsky addresses in his essay "Education and Psychology."

Once, in the course of my research, I developed a mathematical expression I needed to integrate. I had taken freshman calculus at MIT, but that had been a long time ago, so I was unsure what to do. Then I remembered one of Minsky's suggestions: when in doubt, just think about what a program would do. So instead of looking for my calculus textbook, I pulled out James Slagle's symbolic integration program, which he wrote for his thesis that Minsky supervised.[1] The integration problem yielded. Minsky's essay is all about pushing the same kind of idea down to the earliest years of elementary education: let children figure out how to make a program think, and they will have a better understanding of better ways to think because they have been led to think about thinking.

Minsky notes that one powerful idea learned by thinking about thinking is the power of naming and how naming can make us better thinkers. He writes this about feedback: "everyone should know these ideas, but unless we teach people names for them, they'll find it hard to think about such things, or even to learn to recognize them" (essay 6, "Education and Psychology"). My colleague Gerald Sussman, who was another of Minsky's students, promotes the same idea. He says, "When you name something, you get power over it." So once you have *feedback* in your vocabulary, you get power over the feedback idea. I call it the Rumpelstiltskin principle, after the fairy tale in which a miller's daughter gains power over an imp by knowing his name.

Minsky explains that many such powerful ideas—the power of good representation, the notion of state, the divide and conquer idea, what to do when interacting with an adversary—are acquired by way of projects reminiscent of those Seymour Papert and Minsky devised when Papert developed the Logo programming language specifically for children.

Minsky and Papert favored projects involving feedback because it is a powerful idea and because children greatly enjoy programming little robots to follow a track by reducing off-track deviations.[2] Then a little later, the child programmers can see the same difference-reduction idea in Newell-Simon-style problem solvers.[3] The problem solvers apply operators to reduce the difference between where you are in solving a problem and having the problem solved. Then, having thought about difference reduction, given it a name, and noted its power, the children can use the difference-reduction idea themselves when they solve problems. They will have learned something important about how to think.

Other projects Minsky suggests in this essay sometimes seemed beyond the capacity of children younger than PhD age, but that was Minsky being Minsky—often, through conversation, surprising projects were born from his suggestions. He treated everyone the same, totally ignoring their age, gender, and all the other things that do not matter with surprising results.

A decade after Minsky wrote "Education and Psychology," some of the goals he suggested for educational projects, such as object identification, have been achieved by large research groups with massive amounts of computing. Deep neural nets, somewhat unexpectedly, can distinguish between cats and dogs. Minsky's project suggestions remain in force, however, because figuring out how we humans see remains an open and extremely hard problem.

Evidently Minsky believed that perceptual projects could be made easy enough for children to work on; he was less confident about projects involving common sense. But Minsky himself often noted that what seems hard may be easy and vice versa. The cognitive projects Minsky thought to be hard might actually be easier from the perspective of what we have since learned about modeling what we humans do when we listen to and read stories about people and things.[4] Reading this essay on education and psychology led me to wonder how his ideas about teaching thinking might complement my Minsky-inspired thinking about the role of story understanding in setting us humans apart from other animals.

This is what I think: We have common sense, and we can reason, but commonsense reasoning is a special case of recipe following, and recipe following is a special case of storytelling. So let us encourage children not only to understand perception and action better by programming robots but also to understand how stories work by way of projects aimed at thinking about story understanding.

When I was in elementary school, I had a lot of fun diagramming sentences, and the sentence-diagramming exercises taught me a lot about sentence structure. So why not have children diagram stories? Which events cause others? What common sense rules do you need to understand "Goldilocks"? Where do you have to make assumptions? Can you use the story, augmented by common sense, to draw a picture of how the events fit together? How can you recognize concepts, such as revenge, in the picture?

Hand simulation would go a long way; writing programs could come later with something like a Logo-for-working-with-stories language. Children could work on projects aimed at telling stories persuasively, which would help them to understand how to be more persuasive. They would also understand techniques used by others to persuade them. Projects could turn to thinking about how to determine credibility. They could build detectors for fake news. All of this would dovetail nicely with Minsky's suggestion that children learn how magic works. In one case, it is about understanding perceptual trickery; in another, it is about the kind of storytelling trickery we call either telling true stories persuasively or propaganda, depending on which side of an issue we favor. So understanding how stories work might make those children into better voters than many adults. But more important, it might make those children less susceptible, as they grow up, to the stresses of modern life.

As Minsky concludes this essay, he talks about thinking with "My" instead of "I," with the "My" acknowledging that everyone has parts and those parts can have correctable bugs. With "I," he notes, you are a single thing, with no parts you can work on separately. One aspect of this, I think, is that we all have a part that tells stories about ourselves, and that essential part is rarely bug free. We may tell ourselves disparaging stories about ourselves and become depressed. On the other hand, we can tell other kinds of wrong stories and become dangerously narcissistic. What is the cure? Maybe we should have children write programs that tell stories about themselves so that children can see what happens when their programs tell themselves the wrong kind of story. Could they then recognize, and perhaps avoid, the wrong kind of storytelling in themselves?

I have always thought that Minsky's writings are like diamond mines—immensely full of ideas, which when cut and polished, shine refulgently. This essay on education and psychology is a prime example. It is so full of inspiring ideas that it took me several sessions to get through it, all interspersed with excited thinking about implications and what to do next.

Essay 6 Education and Psychology

What goals do we want our schools to achieve? Most parents agree that their children should learn about History, Language, Science and Math, and get some instruction in Health, Sports, and Art. Most parents also want their children taught to behave in what they regard to be civilized ways. And surely, most parents would also agree that schools should help children learn *good ways to think.* However, while schools have good ways to teach facts about subjects, many pupils still fail to build adequate skills for applying that knowledge.*

But if "good thinking" is one of our principal goals, then why don't schools try to explicitly teach about how human Learning and Reasoning work? Instead we tacitly assume that if we simply provide enough knowledge, then each child's brain will "self-organize" appropriate ways to apply those facts. Then would it make sense for us to include a subject called "Human Psychology" as part of the grade-school curriculum? I don't think we can do that yet, because few present-day teachers would agree about which "Theories of Thinking" to teach.

* Thanks to Cynthia Solomon and Gloria Rudisch for many ideas in this essay.

So instead, we'll propose a different approach: *to provide our children with ideas they could use to invent their own theories about themselves!* The rest of this essay will suggest some benefits that could come from this, and some practical ways to accomplish it, by engaging children in various kinds of constructive, computer-related projects.

Why We Can't Yet Include "Psychology" in the Primary School Curriculum

Today's most popular "theories of learning" are based on a century of experiments in which we place a pigeon or rat in a certain situation and reward it with food if it responds with a certain action. Then later, that animal will more often behave in that same way.

> ... Of several responses made to the same situation, those which are ... closely followed by satisfaction to the animal will, other things being equal, be more firmly connected with the situation, so that, when that situation recurs, those responses will be more likely to recur ... while responses followed by discomfort will become less likely to occur.—Edward L. Thorndike 1911

Those experiments also showed that a quicker reward has a larger effect, so educators often use problem sets in which each new task is almost the same as the last. This causes most answers to be correct, which therefore results in more frequent rewards, and this helps to make classrooms more pleasant. Those carefully graded assignments work well to prepare for short-answer tests, but they don't help prepare us for real-world life, where problems don't come in neat sequences.[†]

[†] Later researchers discovered that those effects last much longer when rewards come less predictably. It also turns out that punishment helps

However, this type of learning only works well when the animal can already recognize each such situation or "stimulus" and the required reaction or "response" is already in that animal's repertoire. To ensure these conditions, most classic experiments constrained each animal to choose between only two different buttons to press. Then that reward-based theory of learning worked remarkably well to predict how sub-human animals react to those simplified situations. But that theory only described those animals' external behaviors, their motor responses to sensory inputs. The theory never progressed to shed more light on how people learn to *react in their minds* to more complex problems and situations. ‡

---

to suppress "wrong" responses—but those behaviors can reappear after punishment stops, sometimes even with greater strength—so simply withdrawing reward tends to be more effective. For more details, see http://en.wikipedia.org/wiki/Reinforcement.

In any case, children are different from pigeons and rats. Those classic experiments don't help much to explain how people learn to represent knowledge in their brains and, later, retrieve the information that might be most relevant, so that they can reason, plan, and construct new ideas. When we try to extend those old theories from pigeons to people, we find that they tell us little about the higher-levels of minds that distinguish us from those animals.

More advanced ideas about psychology began to emerge in the 1940s from the new field called Cybernetics, which then evolved into Cognitive Science and Artificial Intelligence. These new sciences are constantly producing new ideas about minds, but the concepts are still changing so fast that they aren't yet stable enough to teach. By default, the ideas from those early years of research on the "external behavior" of animals still dominate the context in which most present-day teachers are taught to teach.

---

‡ This essay uses the term "reward-based" instead of the more common word "reinforcement," which in the infancy of Psychology was meant to suggest that learning strengthens direct "connections" between stimuli and responses. But this is not an adequate image of what happens in human brains, where different processes work at multiple levels to change different structures and representations, in ways that rarely can be observed from watching a person's external behavior. See Section 5 of *The Emotion Machine*.

Some Deficiencies of Behavior-Based Theories

Humans Learn Negative Expertise. We tend to think of knowledge in positive terms, and of "experts" as people who know what to do. But much of an expert's ability comes from knowing about the most common mistakes, and thus, knowing which things one should not do. Thus, much of a person's competence is based on learning to detect *and suppress* unproductive ways to think. Also, an adequate theory of learning should also cover the "reflective skills" that people use to recognize exceptions to generalizations, to eliminate tactics that waste too much time, and more generally, to make longer-range plans and form broader perspectives. In any case, the early behaviorists rarely recognized the importance of "Negative Expertise" because they cannot directly observe how this affects our ways to behave. In particular, when we deal with difficult problems, we often learn more from our failures than from our successes.[§]

[§] See http://web.media.mit.edu/~minsky/papers/NegExp.mss.txt.

Human Minds Make High-Level Credit-Assignments. New situations are seldom the same as previous ones. After you solve a difficult problem, it won't help much to just remember the actions that solved it. You probably had to make many attempts before you found a successful one, and it wouldn't make sense to "reward" all those prior attempts. It sometimes helps to reward your most recent reactions, but generally, it's more important to recognize which earlier strategic decisions should get credit for one's latest success. We briefly discussed this in Essay 3, but also see Section 8-5 of *The Emotion Machine*.[1]

Human Minds Think about What They're Thinking About. After you've "wasted" a lot of time by using a process that finally failed, you usually try to figure out some cause or reason for *why* it failed. However, those older theories never tried to describe the methods that people use for *thinking about what we've been thinking about*. But I'm convinced that these "self-reflective" processes are the principal ones that people use for *developing new ways to think*. I doubt that simply "rewarding success" helps much to promote one's mental development.

> *Psychology Student: But isn't it an established fact that every child is born with a certain IQ—that is, an unchangeable quantity of innate mental ability?*

There is a popular belief that each person's "amount of intelligence" is fixed, because those *IQ* numbers don't usually change very much after early childhood. However, the evidence for this may be biased because of ignoring other important causes for this:

> ... Biographical information on a sample of twenty men of genius suggests that the typical developmental pattern includes as important aspects: (1) a high degree of attention focused upon the child by parents and other adults, expressed in intensive educational measures and, usually, abundant love; (2) isolation from other children, especially outside the family; and (3) a rich efflorescence of fantasy as a reaction to the preceding conditions. ... [If so, then] the mass education of our public school system is, in its way, a vast experiment on the effect of reducing all three factors to a minimum: accordingly, it should tend to suppress the occurrence of genius.—Harold McCurdy, 1960**

** Harold G. McCurdy, "The Childhood Pattern of Genius," *Horizon Magazine*, May 1960, 32–38.

This also could be related to the process we mentioned in Essay 3:

> A new class of 6-year-old children will soon begin to share similar ways to think and behave. Then, next year, when they are 7 years old, most of those pupils will still remain in that group—and thus will tend to perpetuate those same patterns of activity. The next year, they will be 8-year-olds, but will continue to share many attitudes, values, and cognitive strategies. So as those children proceed through their K-12 grades, large portions of their ways to think will remain much like those of 6-year-olds!

Human Thinking Involves Predicting, Comparing, and Planning. The standard reward-based learning schemes envision a pigeon or rat as simply containing a database of two-part rules like *"If the situation is S, Do action R."*[††] But while such rules can describe much of our external behavior, this ignores the fact that you can consider in your mind two actions that you might possibly do. Before you perform any actions at all, you can try to predict the result of each, and then compare those imagined results! This means that to extend our theory from pigeons to people, we'll need to include some *ways to predict the effects of possible actions*.

[††] Some of those rules would be built-in from birth (like "If the light is too bright, then close my eyes") whereas new rules are learned at later times.

However, *If->Do* rules don't predict the results of their actions, we'll also need 3-part *"If->Do->Then.* Here is an example. "If the situation is *S*, and you do *R*, Then situation *T* will result."‡‡ But before the dawn of computers and programs, it was hard to envision such simulations, so those early "Behaviorist" psychologists were forced to ignore the fact that people make longer-range plans and strategies.§§

Human Thinking Is Largely Directed by Goals. You don't open every door you pass, or pick up every object you see. You don't often use an *If->Do* rule unless it serves some current motive or goal. However before the era of Cybernetics, few psychologists tried to make theories about *what goals are and how they work.* Instead, they simply assumed that each animal brain contains a separate set of rules for each of that animal's goals, intentions, motives, or drives—one set of rules to use when hungry and another set to use when angry, etc. Finally in 1957 Allen Newell and Herbert Simon proposed a more constructive theory: a *purposeful* or *goal-based* action is one that results from using a special kind of process (called GPS) that operates on two different descriptions:

---

‡‡ Chapter 5 of *The Emotion Machine* explains how to link sets of these 3-part rules into networks of knowledge that we can use to simulate "virtual worlds" inside our minds, so that we can imagine the sequences of possible actions that we call our "Future Plans."

§§ See the review by Kenneth MacCorquodale reprinted at https://www.ncbi.nlm.nih.gov/pmc/articles/PMC1333660/.

S is a description of the situation that the machine is currently in.

G is a description of a *future* state that the machine "wants" to be in.

GPS is a process that repeatedly looks for a difference between **S** and **G**, and then performs some action on **S** that is likely to lessen that difference.

Such a process will result in behavior that appears to do just what we mean by "pursuing a goal," because it will persist at removing the differences it perceives between "what it has" and "what it wants," unless some other process intervenes to change or remove that **G**.***

*** See Section 6-3 of *The Emotion Machine* for more details about the Newell-Simon idea. Conjecture: it seems likely that, in the brain, such information is represented, at least in part, by the so-called "Mirror Neurons" that Giacomo Rizzolatti has identified.

However, Human Learning Doesn't Always Depend Only on Getting Pleasant Rewards. We can adapt to small changes in familiar conditions by making small changes to skills that we already know. But when thrust into strange environments, we may need to abandon our older techniques. This can lead to unpleasant feelings like pain and grief.[†††]

> Pleasure pursues objects that are beautiful, melodious, fragrant, savory, soft. But curiosity, seeking new experiences, will even seek out the contrary of these, not to experience the discomfort that may come with them, but from a passion for experimenting and knowledge.—Augustine,*Confessions*, Book 10.

> Why do children enjoy the rides in amusement parks, knowing that they will be scared, even sick? Why do explorers endure discomfort and pain—knowing that their very purpose will disperse once they arrive? And what makes people work for years at jobs they hate, so that someday they will be able to—they seem to have forgotten what! ... It is the same for solving difficult problems, or climbing freezing mountain peaks, or playing pipe organs with one's feet: some parts of the mind find these horrible, while other parts enjoy forcing those first parts to work for them.—*The Society of Mind*, Chap. 9.04.

In other words, adventurousness can overcome unpleasantness: when "pleasant" or "positive" rewards fail to help us learn more difficult subjects, we can make ourselves enjoy discomforts and pains, by acquiring what Augustine called "a passion for experimenting and knowledge."

> Citizen: How can you speak of "enjoying" discomfort? Isn't that a self-contradiction?

[†††] Chapter 9 of *The Emotion Machine* discusses some ways to prevent such discomforts from keeping us from learning new things whereas the old reward-based theories ignored what one could call the *"Pleasure of Exploration-Pain."*

This only seems paradoxical when you think of yourself as an entity that can feel only one feeling at a time. But if you imagine your mind as a system that runs a host of concurrent processes, then you can see how some parts of your mind might "enjoy" making other parts "suffer"—as when "it feels good" to have just discovered a new kind of blunder or mistake. In fact, that's exactly what sport coaches teach! Of course, those athletes still feel physical pains, just as artists and scientists feel mental pains. But somehow, they manage to train themselves to keep those pains from spiraling into the awful cascades we call *suffering*.‡‡‡

> *Scientist: Few things bring more pleasure to me than replacing my old ideas, and then showing that my new theories are better than those of my competitors.*
> *Artist: It hurts to discard a hard-earned technique, but nothing surpasses the thrill of conceiving new ways to represent and to think about things.*

1907   1932

‡‡‡ Chapter 3 of *The Emotion Machine* shows why we need to distinguish having pain, hurting, and suffering.

One needs to learn not only what works, but also what to do when failure looms. I don't like that tale of *"The Little Engine that Could"* with its helpless injunction to simply repeat *"I think I can, I think I can."* A better motto would be to think *"perhaps it's time to try something else"* because every setback can offer a chance for a new phase of mental development.

The Traditional Theories Do Not Explain Pleasure. From before the dawn of psychology, everyone has always agreed that pleasant rewards help us to learn, but I've never seen any plausible explanations for this. Here is what may be a new way to explain how "pleasure" works:

> *"Pleasure" is a word we use to describe a process that's used to keep a mind from "changing the subject" of the person's most recent concern. One might need such a function to preserve the current contents of memory for long enough for Credit-Assignment to be accomplished!*

So, while we usually see Pleasure as positive, we also should see it as negative because it suppresses competing activities during the time in which Credit-Assignment proceeds. Similarly, we often need to suppress other interests to keep ourselves working on difficult problems.

But if pleasure has negative aspects, then why does it "feel good" to us? People often answer this by saying that feelings are so basic, simple, and direct that there's nothing much to say about them! However, in Psychology, it's often the case that the things that "seem" simplest turn out to be the ones that are the most complex! In this case, "I feel good" might mean, "Right now, I've suppressed all my other concerns, so all of my problems seem to be gone."

Teaching Cybernetics Instead of Psychology

All this suggests that our ideas about psychology are still developing so rapidly that it wouldn't make sense for us to select any current "theory of thinking" to teach. So instead, we'll propose a different approach: *to provide our children with ideas they could use to invent their own theories about themselves!* The rest of this essay will suggest that such ideas could come from engaging children in projects that involve making machines that have 'lifelike' behaviors. Such projects would engage and integrate many concepts that we separately treat today, in Physics, Biology, and Mathematics—and in Social Studies, Psychology, and Economics—along with other important principles that don't fit into any of those traditional subjects.

A flood of new concepts about what machines could do began to emerge in the 1940s, from research in the field called Cybernetics, which soon then led to other fields called Control Theory, Computer Science, Artificial Intelligence, and Cognitive Psychology. Each of those new sciences brought hosts of new ideas about how to build systems that actually do some of the things we use "thinking" to do. So now, in the spirit of Seymour Papert's "constructionism," we can enable our children to experiment with networks composed of collections of parts that support many sorts of knowledge-based processes.[§§§] This is important because *that's what we are*.

Consequently, it makes sense to expect children to use such ideas to make better ways to think about themselves. We could start by encouraging them to build simplified models of the sensor and motor systems of animals, and put these creatures into environments to experiment, first with each one's separate behavior, and then with the social relations in groups of them.

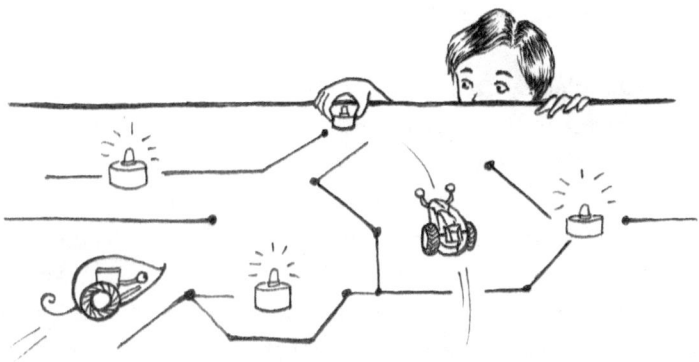

Do we have enough evidence that such experiments will improve those children's self-images? Our answer must be ambiguous: in the past we've seen many cases in which such experiments appeared to work well, but those LOGO-based projects were never extended to large enough scales. But such projects are far more feasible today, because equipment is now so much cheaper.

[§§§] See http://en.wikipedia.org/wiki/Constructionist_learning.

Some critics might complain that subjects like Cybernetics and Computer Science do not deserve a special place in the elementary school curriculum, because they are too specialized. However, Computer Science is not only about computers themselves; more generally, it provides us with a whole new world of ways to understand complex processes, including the ones that go on in our own mind. For until those new techniques arrived (such as *programming languages* for describing processes, and *data structures* for representing knowledge), we had no expressions that people could use to articulate and communicate good new ideas about such things.****

Understanding Systems with Feedback Loops. While rule-based systems work well to explain much of how other species behave, human beings do much more than directly react to "Situations" or "Stimuli." For example (as in the GPS systems we mention above), we often make mental comparisons between (1) the real-world situation that we are actually "in" and (2) some "goal-situation" we'd prefer to be in. *Then we can use our descriptions of those differences to decide which of the actions would most likely help us to achieve that goal.*

Now, this might seem so obvious as to make you wonder why I'm repeating it. But myself, I've often wondered why this idea wasn't clear to the early Behaviorists! For if we adopt this process-based concept of what goals are, this changes our view

---

**** On the surface, Computer Science may seem to resemble Mathematics, but one can see it as complementary: Mathematics provides us with complex ways to look more deeply into seemingly simple things—whereas Computer Science tends to give us simpler ways to think about more complicated things.

of our own behaviors: *we react less to Situations themselves, than to their Differences to our goals!*

In other words, if we think in terms of goal-based processes, we can see our actions as mainly resulting from "feedback loops" that work to change differences rather than things. Of course it is perfectly obvious that some such loops increase differences, while others tend to reduce them. It also is not very hard to see that when feedback *increases* differences, this can lead to exponential growth (which can never be sustained for long, because it will soon exhaust some resource). It's only a little harder to see why, when feedback *reduces* differences, this can make a process more stable and reliable. However, it also turns out that there is an astonishing range of phenomena that come from systems that lie between those extremes, and the study of such processes was what led to the new science called Cybernetics. For example, when feedback-loops have time-delays, this can lead to repetitive oscillations, or even to the complex phenomena that mathematicians describe as "chaotic."

In any case, virtually every real-world system includes some of those kinds of feedback loops, so it seems to me that everyone should know these ideas, but unless we teach people names for them, they'll find it hard to think about such things, or even to learn to recognize them. An easy way to learn about feedback loops is to make (or better, to simulate) a turtle-like robot that follows a line on the floor, by detecting when the line is to the right or left, and using that information for steering.[††††]

[††††] See more discussions of feedback systems in http://en.wikipedia.org/wiki/Feedback, http://en.wikipedia.org/wiki/Control_theory, and http://www.well.com/~abs/curriculum.html. Note that the Newell-Simon theory of goals can be seen as a negative feedback process.

That basic idea is simple enough, but soon the child will find that the system is likely to get off the track (because of excessive overshoot, or by encountering an obstacle). Then the child can invent various ways to prevent or recover from this (say, by discovering ways to search for it). Also, in the case of objects that move, one can invent many different ways to try to track and predict their future paths. But this opens the door to another whole world: our child might now want to go further, to make this animal try to predict and pursue another one that also moves, or even one that is trying to escape! Then, wow, we've suddenly entered the social realm!

Other Suggestions for Cybernetics Projects

It would take a whole book to begin to discuss the range of new concepts that emerged in the 1950s from combining ideas from Psychology, Cybernetics, and other sciences. I don't see any tidy way to organize this huge body of knowledge, so the rest of this essay will only list a number of different approaches for this.[3] First are some ideas for specific projects.

Robotic Projects. Most present-day robotic projects use wheeled vehicles for mobility, because these are so easy to build. However,

Education and Psychology

I'd like to see more projects that try to design robots that walk, because they would be more versatile. It's not very difficult to make 4-legged walking machines, while 2-legged ones are much harder to stabilize. But once you can keep them from falling down, you can go on to make them jump and run! And of course, there's a whole new world of ideas that will come from building micro-worlds in which several such creatures interact; you could either control them all from a central place, or just give them some ways to communicate.[2]

Simulated vs. Physical Robots. It is remarkable how engaged people become when they first see mechanical, physical robots. But eventually, our students learn more by working with computer programs that simulate robots, because then one can better design and control one's experiments. A trouble with physical robots is that too much of the students' time is consumed with trivial bugs that are hard to fix; also, it is hard to control enough of the robot's environment to make the results reproducible. To make good use of our young people's time, we'll need to provide them with "virtual" physical worlds that work quickly and realistically.

However, we also should note that in recent years, increasingly fewer children have developed skills for making and fixing mechanical things, because so few products today are repairable. So building physical robots can be an excellent way to remedy this growing helplessness, and one can find many robot construction kits with a Google search for "robot kits." However, there are advantages to learning to build machines using general-purpose construction sets, such as Erector, TinkerToy, and Fischertechnik—but these are becoming hard to get. LEGO is more widely available, but is generally less versatile. The next few years will bring new sorts of fabrication techniques, e.g., 3-D printers, which today are still too expensive for schools. But still, there's nothing wrong with learning some old-fashioned carpentry!

Balancing and Manipulation. Build a moving hand that can balance a stick, first in one and then in two dimensions. Try to discover the limitations of such processes. Try to build a juggling machine. I don't know of any projects that have made machines that can tie a knot or button a shirt.

Optimization and Problem Solving. To recognize a particular object from a collection of several things, one will need some way to determine which of them best fits a certain description. A powerful method for solving such problems is to describe things in terms of coordinates, parameters, or variables, and then to find "the path of steepest ascent." Such "hill-climbing" programs can often provide us with numerical ways to "optimize" things when our more clever symbolic methods fail (as they most often will, in everyday life).

Visual Recognition Projects. One example is recognizing printed and handwritten characters and words. Why is it easier to recognize an entire word than to recognize the letters that make it? Can you make a program that will distinguish pictures of cats from pictures of dogs? (I don't know of any successful such project.)[4] There do exist programs that do well at recognizing faces, but I've not yet heard of any program that can look at a picture of a typical room and identify the most common types of objects in view. One problem is that the appearance of an object will depend on one's point of view, so the programmer will need to invent some concepts to deal with this. So these kinds of projects can demonstrate the importance of making appropriate kinds of abstractions.

Processing Voices and Other Sounds. One can also learn a lot about perceptual processes by making programs that classify features of everyday sounds. Can you design a program to distinguish the tones of a violin, trumpet, and clarinet? How far can you get toward recognizing such everyday sounds as footsteps, voices, the clinks of cups and plates, coughs, crumpling paper, etc? Could children invent better tricks for this than the ones that most engineers would use? Experiment with grammars and parsing procedures. Then take any other project we've mentioned here and add an interface to it so that you can control it by using verbal commands.

Performance Systems. Some children might like to make a program that can read a Music score, and then actually perform the music. Or try to experiment with phonetics to make a program that reads a story aloud. This would lead to all sorts of ideas about pronunciation, accent, stress, and up to the study of rhetoric.

Puzzles and Game-Playing Programs. Write a program to do your math homework (and see if your teacher will accept the results) or write programs to solve such spatial puzzles as Tangrams, Pentominos, Magic Squares, or Crossword-like puzzles, etc. Many children become so addicted to playing particular games that this can become a serious problem. However, we might be able to exploit this by encouraging children to try to write "front end" programs to play existing games, or to design and program their own new games.

Cognitive Projects. How difficult would it be to make a system that does some humanlike commonsense reasoning? Answer: this would be very hard, indeed: in fact, it is at the forefront of current research in Artificial Intelligence. Nevertheless, it would be interesting for children to see how much they can do, using Logic alone, and then to add other forms of reasoning—for example, by using analogies. And any such project could be improved by enabling it to improve itself, by adding abilities to learn. For example, each part of a system might be improved by adding a reinforcement-based neural network to it.

Theories about Finite-State Machines. Modern Computer Science includes a great collection of useful ideas about different kinds of processes, many of which can be built into systems that even young children could make and then "play" with. These could include simple logical reasoning systems, or machines that do arithmetic, or ones that play some popular games. One productive way to begin would be to experiment with networks of logical *AND*s, *OR*s, and *NOT*s. Indeed, a good way to learn about computers might be to begin with such "logical networks" instead of conventional programming languages because this yields different insights into what computers are and how they work. ‡‡‡‡In any case, if our goal is to attract children to technical concepts, this 'finite state' approach might turn out to be more productive (and more enjoyable) than making them learn Arithmetic.§§§§

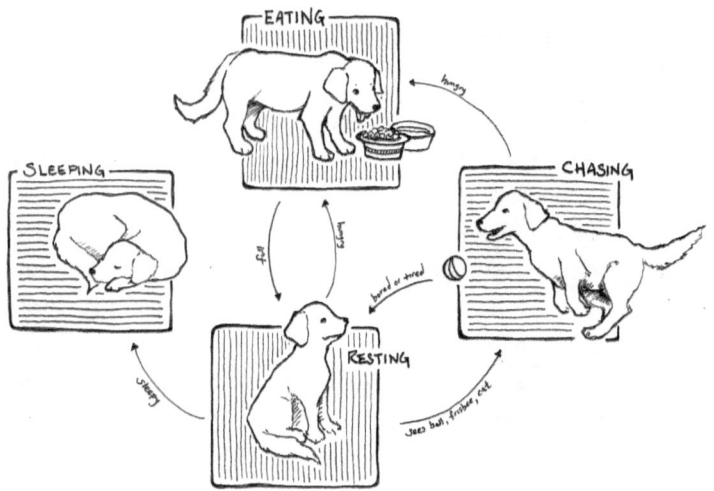

‡‡‡‡ Also, building so-called "Expert Systems" provides another interesting alternative to conventional programming. See http://en.wikipedia.org/wiki/Expert_system.

§§§§ In this approach to Mathematics, one doesn't need to memorize those arithmetic tables that some children take hundreds of hours to learn. Few adults recollect how long a single hour can seem to a six-year-old child—and this could be one more reason why so many adults loathe mathematics. See http://www.triviumpursuit.com/articles/research_on_teaching_math.php.

Education and Psychology

Learning "Critical Thinking." This may seem somewhat out of place, but I want to recommend encouraging every child to learn a number of magic tricks because (1) this is a good introduction to "the psychology of perception" and (2) it also leads to important insights about how what we perceive is affected by context, expectation, and deception. For children who can't get lessons from local magicians, it would be good to have some online magic-teaching programs.[5]

How It Can Help to Think of Oneself as a Machine

Many people are firmly convinced that to have a mechanical image of oneself must lead to a depressing sense of helplessness—because it means that you're doomed to remain what you are, and there's nothing that you can do about this. However, I'll argue exactly the opposite: seeing yourself as a kind of machine can be a liberating idea—because *whatever you might dislike about yourself, that might be caused by a bug you could fix!* For example, contrast these pairs of self-images:

> *I'm not good at math.—There are some bugs in my symbolic processes.*
> *I'm just not very smart.—Some of my programs need improvements.*
> *I don't like this subject.——My current goals need better priorities.*
> *I am confused.——Some of my processes may conflict with others.*

If you think of yourself in terms of "I," then you'll see yourself as a single thing, which has no parts to change or rearrange. But using "My" can help you to envision yourself as composed of parts, which could enable you to imagine specific changes that might improve your ways to think. In other words, if you can represent your mind as made of potentially repairable machinery, then you can think about remedies. For example, you might be able to diagnose some bugs or deficiencies in the apparatus that you use for everyday functions like these:

> *Time-management.——Organizing Searches.——Splitting problems into parts.*
> *Selecting good ways to represent things.——Making appropriate cognitive maps.*
> *Allocating short-term memory.——Making appropriate Credit-Assignments.*

It seems clear that some children are better than others at doing this kind of "self reflection." Could this be a skill that we could teach? Perhaps, but this might not yet be practical because we don't yet know enough about our human mental machinery. However, the types of projects this essay recommends could help us to promote that goal, by giving our children more tools to use for constructing better views of themselves!

Learning to Draw

Margaret Minsky

Marvin makes three points in these essays. The first is that role models and mentors, which Marvin terms *imprimers*, are of paramount importance. Assimilating the ways that other people think is fundamental to becoming a good thinker. The second is that thinking about one's own thinking and making explicit cognitive maps of what one learns ought to be included in children's education. The third is that one should have the opportunity to become an expert early in one's life, in high school or even elementary school, as Marvin himself had. Let's reflect more closely on his areas of early expertise. They developed with him throughout his life.

In 1993, Marvin wrote:

> A familiar experience for me was to learn to recognize new families of patterns. When first you see the circuits of a radio or a television set, it seems a hopeless jumble of symbols and lines; later, when one understands, one sees the structures and functions together as though it were perfectly obvious. *It happens with drawings, and music, and mathematics*, and even with politics and social affairs. As our pattern recognition skills improve, things become more real than reality until, eventually, one sees perfectly clearly many things that aren't there at all.[1]

"*It happens with drawings, and music, and mathematics.*" These are three areas in which Marvin became expert in childhood, and

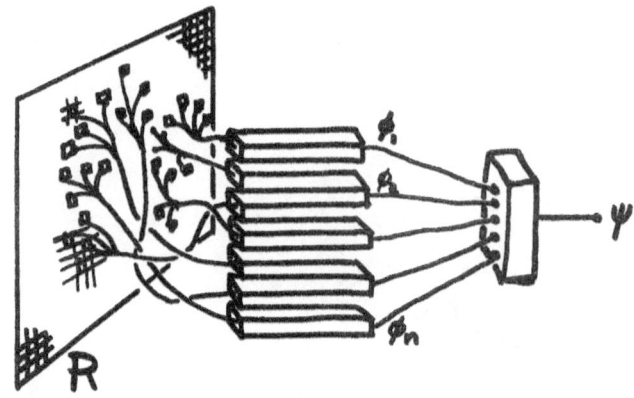

Figure 7.1
Marvin Minsky's hand-drawn Perceptrons figure for Draft MIT AI Memo 140

again in high school, and again in college. He did not stop there but revisited each of those areas of expertise with significant projects in his thirties and forties and, at least for music and drawing, for the rest of his life.

He told stories about drawing, music, and mathematics from all of those eras. He was considered a musical prodigy at an early age and a top mathematician in middle and high school. Surprisingly, given many early successes and achievements, he only felt he came into his true power as a mathematician during his work on the theory of *Perceptrons*, written with Seymour Papert and published as a book in 1969. I watched that book happen. He drew all of its illustrations by hand, and I watched him become expert, again, in drawing. It was then that he came into his own as an illustrator, working night and day, using and learning a new set of drawing tools, as different from his high school and college tools as a new musical instrument.

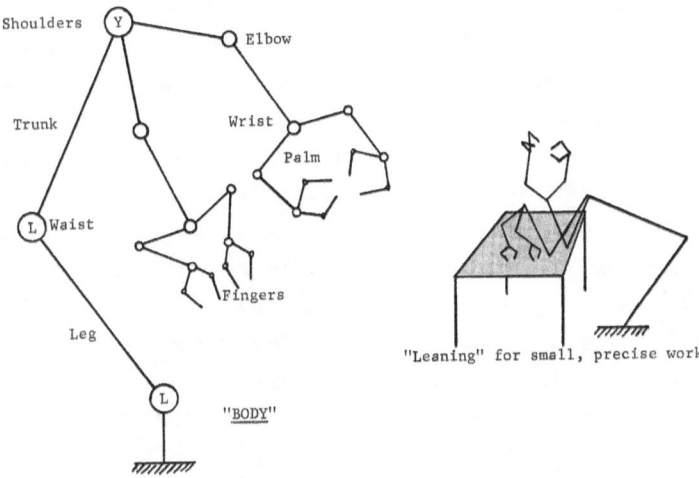

Figure 7.2

The point is that he had become expert in drawing several times by then, using tools of the day with varying purposes, just as he delved into being a mathematical expert early and often.

He mentions being spellbound as a child by a book by Henrik Van Loon, who illustrated his own books. I bet they were imprimers for his own style in later childhood and onward. He recalled taking mechanical drawing classes in high school and loving them. Figure 7.2 is a binary tree robot he invented and drew in 1965. During his early career he drew many schematics and technical drawings for electronics, robots, and sketched ideas. He showed this robot to Stanley Kubrick, as an advisor to Kubrick's movie *2001*; you can see its influence in the manipulator arms of the movie's space pods.

When it came time for the *Perceptrons* illustrations, he set up a studio in his living room at home. One desk was devoted to the large sheets of vellum, and a nearby table to the complicated new

Rapidograph pens with tiny syringe-like points and their filler ink bottles, cleaning solutions, soaking cups, whiteout, and other paraphernalia. Figures 7.3a and b are drawings of a similar set of Rapidograph pens. They had a test-tube-like stand to hold all the sizes. The tiny tips went down to size 0, 00, and 000, which was all of 0.25 mm wide. More time was spent loading the pens, cleaning them, and keeping them from drying out in order to get ink lines of various widths than actually drawing. The rest of the table was filled with templates, straightedges, french curves, and Letrasets, though in the end, the drawings were all freehand, including numerals and lettering. He drew 172 illustrations for the original 246-page *Perceptrons* book (see figures 7.4a–d). As in the book you are holding, there was an illustration on almost every page, and two on many pages!

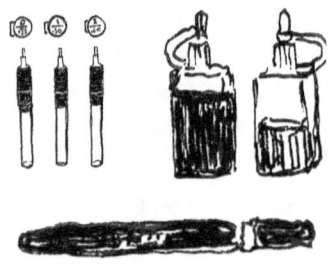

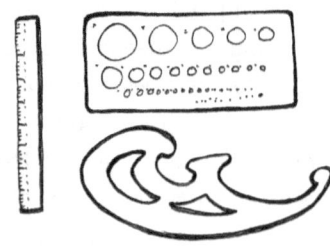

Figure 7.3a   **Figure 7.3b**

Learning to Draw

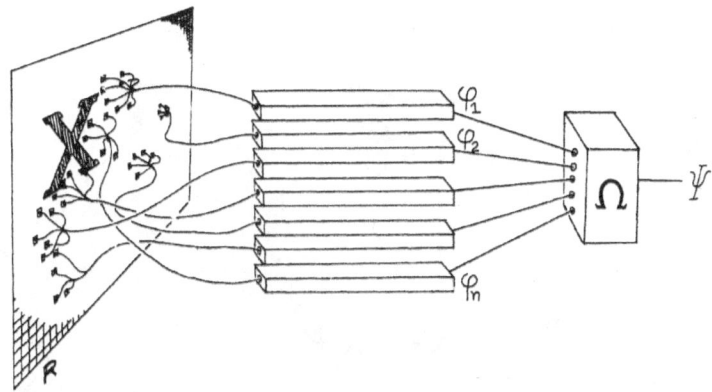

Figure 7.4a

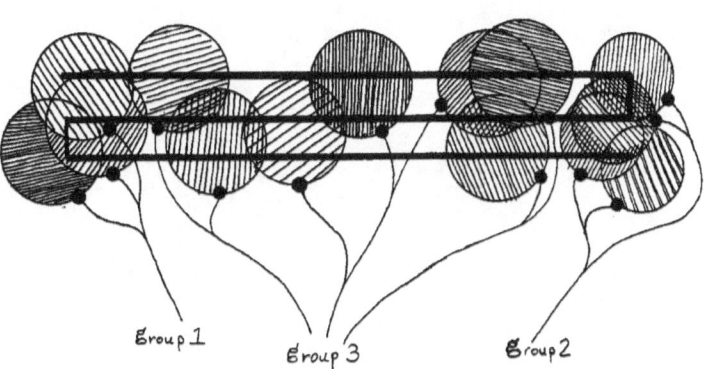

Figure 7.4b

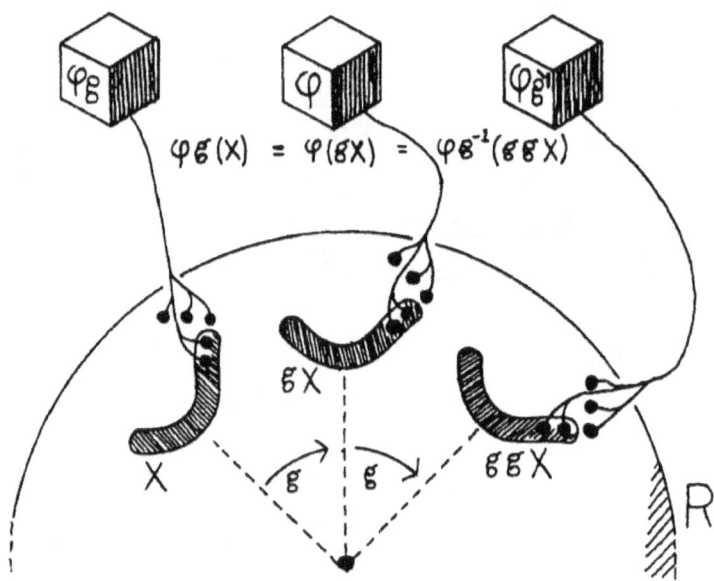

Figure 7.4c

Learning to Draw

Then C_0 can be removed from H_1 by a series of deformations in which, first, H_1 is drawn to the periphery

and then C_0 is temporarily attached:

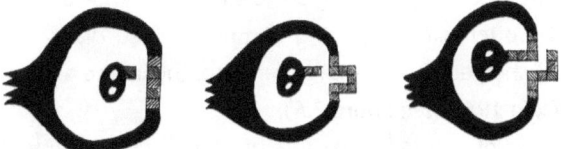

Notice that this does not change the value of $G(X)$. Also, since it reduces both C and H by unity, it does not change $E(X) = C(X) - H(X)$.

We can then swing C_1 around to the outside and reconnect to obtain

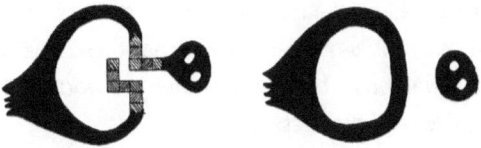

Figure 7.4d

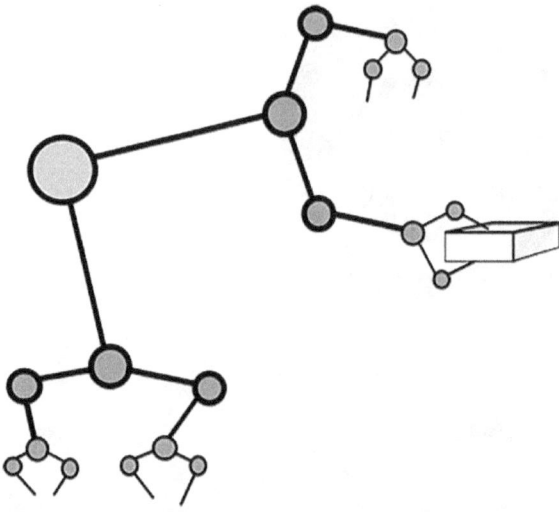

Figure 7.5

In 2006, Marvin gave a talk at the Coolidge Corner Theater *Science on Screen* series, preceding a showing of the movie *2001*. By that time, he often sketched using computer-aided diagramming tools, and he showed his own re-rendering of the image he showed Kubrick back in 1965 (see figure 7.5).

This glimpse of a little-known side of Marvin raises many questions. How did his own relationship with drawing tie into his more general ideas about learning and education? What role did drawing or graphic thinking have in the development of his ideas about computation and intelligence? What can be said about his methods or approach to teaching himself a new skill? What attracted him to drawing in the first place? It is not certain whether these questions are answerable in a literal sense, but perhaps they are worth reflecting on now that you've read these essays.

Contributors

Hal Abelson is a Professor of Electrical Engineering and Computer Science at MIT, a fellow of the IEEE, and a founding director of the Creative Commons and the Free Software Foundation. He directed the first implementation of Logo for Apple II, coordinated the MIT OpenCourseWare initiative, served as cochair of the MIT Council on Education Technology, and is a former director of the Center for Democracy and Technology. He leads the development of MIT App Inventor.

Walter Bender is the former director of the MIT Media Lab (2000–2006) and the MIT Media Lab's Electronic Publishing Group (1985–2006). He helped launch One Laptop per Child in 2006, and in 2008 founded the nonprofit organization Sugar Labs, where he currently serves as the executive director.

Alan Kay, in 1968, while a doctoral student at the University of Utah, built a cardboard prototype of the Dynabook, "a personal computer for children of all ages." In 1970 he joined Xerox PARC, where he advanced the development of graphical user interfaces and Ethernet technologies, and led the development of Smalltalk and the Alto computer. He has served as

Chief Scientist at Atari, Senior Apple Fellow (Vivarium Project), Vice President of Research and Development at the Walt Disney Company, and Senior Fellow at Hewlett Packard Labs. In 2001, he founded Viewpoints Research Institute, where Squeak and eToys were developed.

Margaret Minsky creates multimedia artifacts exploring learning, improvisation, and thought. Her recent investigations concern embodied interaction with technology aimed at increasing cognitive, social, and physical well-being. She recently completed a residency at the ATLAS Center, an interdisciplinary laboratory at the University of Colorado Boulder. She developed the first technique for creating haptic textures as part of her doctoral research at the MIT Media Lab. Dr. Minsky previously directed research at Atari Cambridge Research and Interval Research Corporation.

Brian Silverman has been involved in the design and development of learning environments for children since he was an MIT undergraduate in the 1970s. He continued this work by designing dozens of Logo versions (including LogoWriter and MicroWorlds), Scratch, LEGO robotics, TurtleArt, and the PicoCricket. Brian has been a Visiting Scientist at the MIT Media Lab, enjoys recreational math, and is a computer scientist and master tinkerer. He once even built a tic-tac-toe playing computer out of Tinkertoys. He is currently the president of the Playful Invention Company.

Cynthia Solomon created Logo, the first programming language for children, along with Wally Feurzeig and Seymour Papert at Bolt, Beranek and Newman. She and Papert continued Logo research at the MIT Artificial Intelligence Lab where the Logo environment was extended to music and robotics with the collaboration of Marvin Minsky. She received her EdD at Harvard University in 1985 and was awarded both the National Center for Women & Information Technology Pioneer Award and the Constructionism Lifetime Achievement Award in 2016.

Gary Stager is one of the world's leading experts and advocates for learning-by-doing, computer programming, and robotics in classrooms. Gary is the founder of the Constructing Modern Knowledge summer institute for educators and is coauthor of *Invent to Learn: Making, Tinkering, and Engineering in the Classroom*. His writings have appeared in (among other places) the *New York Times*, the *Huffington Post*, the *Wall Street Journal*, and *Wired*.

Mike Travers is a software engineer and data architect in the San Francisco Bay Area. He has played a lead role in a variety of software companies building knowledge-based computational tools for the life sciences, including drug discovery, synthetic biology, clinical informatics, and genomic medicine applications.

Mike holds degrees in mathematics and media arts and sciences from MIT, where he did research on artificial life, learning environments, and agent-based computing at the Media Lab. His work focuses on the intersection of knowledge representation, visualization, and discovery. An experienced interaction designer, he has exhibited interactive installations at the SIGGRAPH Art Show and the Boston Computer Museum. He has held research positions at the MIT AI Lab, IBM, SRI, and the Centre Mondial in Paris.

Patrick Henry Winston is Ford Professor of Artificial Intelligence and MacVicar Faculty Fellow at MIT. His Genesis research group focuses on developing a computational account of human intelligence and how human intelligence differs from that of other species, with special attention to modeling human story comprehension.

Xiao Xiao holds a degree in Computer Science from MIT, and completed her Masters and PhD at the MIT Media Lab in 2016. Drawing from her training as a classical pianist, she created music learning technologies for her doctorate that focused on the role of the body in the development of the musical mind.

Xiao currently designs multimedia art installations and continues to pursue learning-related research as an affiliate of the Media Lab and at UPMC (University Pierre and Marie Curie), Paris, France. New installations will be on permanent exhibit at the Historic New Orleans Collection in 2019.

To reflect on her own learning, Xiao began teaching herself how to play the theremin in 2017, inventing new techniques inspired by her experiences with the piano, coding, interaction design, drawing, yoga, and dance. As a thereminist, she has performed at venues such as the Music Box Village in New Orleans and Joe's Pub in New York.

Notes

Preface

1. Marvin elaborates on the importance of computer science:

    I think that Computer Science is the most important thing that's happened since the invention of writing. Fifty years ago, in the 1950s, human thinkers learned for the first time how to describe complicated machines. We invented something called computer programming language, and for the first time people had a way to describe complicated processes and systems, systems made of thousands of little parts all connected together: Before 1950 there were no languages that people could use to exchange ideas about such complex things.

    Why is that important to understand? Because that's what we are: each human individual *is* a complex network of machines! So, Computer Science is important, but that importance has little to do with computers themselves; Computer Science is a new philosophy about complicated processes, about life (both artificial and natural) and about intelligence (also both artificial and natural). It can help us understand our brain. It can help us understand how we learn and what knowledge is.

    (From a public lecture delivered at the Artificial Life V conference in Nara, Japan, May 16, 1996. [Transcription by Nicholas Gessler.])

2. Marvin Minsky, *The Society of Mind* (New York: Simon & Schuster, 1986); Marvin Minsky, *The Emotion Machine: Commonsense Thinking, Artificial Intelligence, and the Future of the Human Mind* (New York: Simon & Schuster, 2006).

3. Seymour Papert, "You Can't Think about Thinking without Thinking about Thinking about Something," *Contemporary Issues in Technology and Teacher Education* 5, no. 3/4 (2005): 366–367, https://eric.ed.gov/?id=EJ1080976.

4. Minsky, *Society of Mind*.

5. Cynthia Solomon, Margaret Minsky, and Brian Harvey, *LogoWorks: Challenging Programs in Logo* (New York: McGraw-Hill, 1986).

6. Here is a memorable excerpt from Mike Travers's 2016 blog post entitled "Firing Up the Emotion Machine" (http://omniorthogonal.blogspot.com/2016/01/firing-up-emotion-machine.html):

> He was I suppose a reductionist, but to label him that is to reduce his own complicated way of thought to a single-word slogan. And that was one kind of reduction he did not practice. His other big trick was to know that there is no one big trick to the mind, that single-idea solutions like logic or bayesianism are insufficient, and that building a mind requires the complex orchestration of multiple mechanisms. *Society of Mind* was itself structured as a cooperating network of very specific ideas for mechanisms, making the form match its content. ... So he tried to take intractable concepts like selves and consciousness and "reduce" them to a complex interaction between mechanisms.

Introduction

1. "The mission of One Laptop per Child (OLPC) is to empower the children of developing countries to learn by providing one connected laptop to every school-age child" (http://laptop.org/en/vision/mission/index.shtml).

2. Dylan Hadfield-Menell, Anca Dragan, Pieter Abbeel, and Stuart Russell, "Cooperative Inverse Reinforcement Learning," in *Proceedings of the 30th International Conference on Neural Information Processing Systems* (Barcelona: ACM, 2016), 3916–3924, https://papers.nips.cc/paper/6420-cooperative-inverse-reinforcement-learning.pdf.

3. Jean Lave and Etienne Wenger, *Situated Learning: Legitimate Peripheral Participation* (Cambridge, UK: Cambridge University Press, 2016). Also see https://en.wikipedia.org/wiki/Community_of_practice.

4. Quoted in Walter Bender, Charles Kane, Jody Cornish, and Neal Donahue, *Learning to Change the World: The Social Impact of One Laptop Per Child* (New York: Palgrave Macmillan, 2012).

5. Seymour Papert, *Mindstorms: Children, Computers, and Powerful Ideas* (New York: Basic Books, 1980).

Essay 1

1. Marvin Minsky, "Preface," in *LogoWorks: Challenging Programs in Logo* (New York: McGraw Hill, 1986), viii-xii.

2. A. Kee Dewdney, *The Tinkertoy Computer* (New York: Freeman, 1993).

3. Since this essay was written, a merged Meccano-Erector set is available. A nice website for history is http://www.girdersandgears.com/.

4. The example here is Kresge Auditorium, designed by Eero Saarinen, whose form is one-eighth of a sphere's surface.

5. Logo Computer Systems, Inc.

Afterword to Essay 1

1. Marvin Minsky, *The Society of Mind* (New York: Simon & Schuster, 1985), 18.

2. Seymour Papert, "Hard Fun," *Bangor Daily News*, 2002, accessed April 23, 2018, http://www.papert.org/articles/HardFun.html.

3. Seymour Papert, *Mindstorms: Children, Computers, and Powerful Ideas* (New York: Basic Books, 1980).

4. See https://gpblocks.org/.

5. GP's usual colorful Tinkertoy-like "blocks" will be shown as "text on gray" for this chapter in black and white.

6. Quite a bit of the substance of this talk was later written up by Marvin in 1970 as his Turing Award Lecture called "Form and Content in Computer Science," published in the *Journal for the Association of Computing*

Machinery 17, no. 2 (April 1970), http://web.media.mit.edu/~minsky/papers/TuringLecture/TuringLecture.html.

Introductory Remarks to Essay 2

1. A fugue is a type of musical composition featuring two or more interweaving voices that take turns stating a musical theme, called the subject. It is a type of contrapuntal music, which consists of several independent melodic lines rather than a single melody and accompaniment. To hear examples of fugues, see the Well-Tempered Clavier (Johann Sebastian Bach, *Bach's Well-Tempered Clavier: 48 Preludes and Fugues for Piano* [London: New York: Music Sales; Amsco Music Pub. Co., 1972]) at http://www2.nau.edu/tas3/wtc.html, and The Art of Fugue by J. S. Bach (Johann Sebastian Bach, *Die Kunst der Fuge: BWV 1080: Autograph, Originaldruck* [Mainz; New York: Schott, 1979]).

2. Seymour Papert, "Powerful Ideas in Mind-Size Bites," in *Mindstorms: Children, Computers, and Powerful Ideas* (New York: Basic Books, 1980), 135–155; Andrea A. diSessa, "Thematic Chapter: Epistemology and Systems Design," in *Computers and Exploratory Learning*, ed. Andrea A. diSessa, Celia Hoyles, Richard Noss, with Laurie D. Edwards (Berlin: Springer, 1993), 15–29.

Essay 2

1. Mathematics is broad and deep. It has a lot of major areas such as algebra and geometry. In this essay Marvin makes mention of a lot of other areas and concepts that may be unfamiliar to a lot of readers. He is trying to make a point. School has chosen a particular slice of mathematics, a fairly small slice. The choice is largely historical and in fact seems a little arbitrary. Marvin is suggesting other slices as the parts of math that schools could introduce. Recently we saw the dawn of mathematics related to computation, which has also introduced new slices. Marvin, in this essay, provides a lot of concrete suggestions for where our focus can be, even if some of it appears foreign right now.

2. At the time he was a computer science graduate student at MIT.

3. Minsky's suggestions are good areas for research.

4. Marvin Minsky, *The Emotion Machine: Commonsense Thinking, Artificial Intelligence, and the Future of the Human Mind* (New York: Simon & Schuster, 2006). Also see essay 1 in this volume.

5. Note Added 24 March 2008

The U.S. Department of Education issued a 90-page report proposing 45 improvements to math education. This report makes almost all the mistakes that I complained about in this memo. Its most emphatic recommendation:

> A major goal for K–8 mathematics education should be proficiency with fractions (including decimals, percents, and negative fractions), for such proficiency is foundational for algebra and, at the present time, seems to be severely underdeveloped. Proficiency with whole numbers is a necessary precursor for the study of fractions, as are aspects of measurement and geometry.

The report says almost nothing about using computers except to suggest that learning to program may bring some benefits "if students' programming is carefully guided by teachers so as to explicitly teach students to achieve specific mathematical goals." Warning: the full report is likely to make your mind throw up. See it at http://www.ed.gov/about/bdscomm/list/mathpanel/report/final-report.pdf.

Introductory Remarks to Essay 3

1. Seymour Bernard Sarason, *The Predictable Failure of Educational Reform: Can We Change Course before It's Too Late?* (San Francisco: Jossey-Bass, 1991); Seymour Bernard Sarason, *Revisiting the Culture of School and the Problem of Change* (New York: Teachers College Press, 1996); Seymour Bernard Sarason, *A Self-Scrutinizing Memoir* (New York: Teachers College Press, 2003); and Seymour Bernard Sarason, *And What Do You Mean by Learning?* (Portsmouth, NH: Heinemann, 2004).

2. Jean Piaget, *Science of Education and the Psychology of the Child* (New York: Orion Press, 1970).

3. L. S. Vygotskiĭ, Michael Cole, Sally Stein, and Allan Sekula, *Mind in Society: The Development of Higher Psychological Processes* (Cambridge, MA: Harvard University Press, 1978); Lev Vygotsky, *Thought and Language*,

ed. and trans. Eugenia Hanfmann, Gertrude Vakar, and Alex Kozulin, rev. and exp. ed. (Cambridge, MA: MIT Press, 2012); and Jean Lave and Etienne Wenger, *Situated Learning: Legitimate Peripheral Participation* (Cambridge, UK: Cambridge University Press, 1991).

4. Seymour Papert, "Hard Fun," *Bangor Daily News*, 2002, accessed February 12, 2018, http://www.papert.org/articles/HardFun.html.

Essay 3

1. "In everyday life, we routinely use terms like *Suffering, Pleasure, Enjoyment,* and *Grief*—but get stuck when we try to explain what these mean. The trouble comes, I think, because we think of such 'feelings' as simple or basic, whereas each one involves intricate processes. For example, I suspect that what we call *'Pleasure'* is involved with the methods we use to identify *which of our recent activities should get credit for our recent successes*" (Marvin Minsky, *The Emotion Machine: Commonsense Thinking, Artificial Intelligence, and the Future of the Human Mind* [New York: Simon & Schuster, 2006], 49).

2. Allen Newell, "The Chess Machine: An Example of Dealing with a Complex Task by Adaptation," in *Proceedings of the Western Joint Computer Conference* (Los Angeles: ACM, 1955), 101–108.

3. See http://www.ou.edu/tulsa/education/faculty-staff.

Introductory Remarks to Essay 4

1. Seymour Papert, "Foreword: The Gears of My Childhood," in *Mindstorms: Children, Computers, and Powerful Ideas* (New York: Basic Books, 1980), vi–viii.

2. Marvin Minsky, "Music, Mind, and Meaning," *Computer Music Journal* 5, no. 3 (1981): 28–44, https://www.musicmindandmeaning.org/.

3. Marvin Minsky, *The Society of Mind* (New York: Simon and Schuster, 1986).

Essay 4

1. This is discussed more extensively in essay 2.

2. A popular view is fixed mindset vs. growth mindset. See Carol Dweck, *Mindset: The New Psychology of Success* (New York: Random House, 2006).

3. Marvin Minsky, "Thinking," in *The Emotion Machine: Commonsense Thinking, Artificial Intelligence, and the Future of the Human Mind* (New York: Simon & Schuster, 2006), 215–253.

4. Marvin discusses reasoning by analogy in detail. See Marvin Minsky, *The Emotion Machine: Commonsense Thinking, Artificial Intelligence, and the Future of the Human Mind* (New York: Simon & Schuster, 2006), 206–209.

5. Just for fun search for "mnemonic examples" on Google and see the multitude of memory aids.

6. For examples of "debugging" applied to stilt-walking and juggling, see Seymour Papert, "Languages for Computers and for People," in *Mindstorms: Children, Computers, and Powerful Ideas* (New York: Basic Books, 1980), 95–119.

7. Dan Ariely, *Predictably Irrational: The Hidden Forces That Shape Our Decisions* (New York: Harper, 2008).

8. Minsky, *The Emotion Machine*.

9. These ideas connect to current discussions on "deliberate practice." See Anders Ericsson and Robert Pool, *Peak: Secrets from the New Science of Expertise* (New York: Houghton Mifflin Harcourt, 2016).

10. Minsky, *The Emotion Machine*, 81, 174, 210.

11. See the Scratch website at https://scratch.mit.edu/ for an example of a well-moderated online community.

Introductory Remarks to Essay 5

1. Marvin Minsky, *The Emotion Machine: Commonsense Thinking, Artificial Intelligence, and the Future of the Human Mind* (New York: Simon & Schuster, 2006).

2. Seymour Papert and Cynthia Solomon, "Twenty Things to Do with a Computer (Artificial Intelligence Memo no. 248 and Logo Memo no. 3, AI Laboratory, MIT, June 1971).

3. Steve Lohr, "As Coding Boot Camps Close, the Field Faces a Reality Check," *New York Times*, August 24, 2017.

4. The Hour of Code is "a global movement reaching tens of millions of students in 180+ countries. Anyone, anywhere can organize an Hour of Code event. One-hour tutorials are available in over 45 languages. No experience needed. Ages 4 to 104" (https://hourofcode.com).

5. Pasi Sahlberg, *Finnish Lessons: What Can the World Learn from Educational Change in Finland?* (New York: Teachers College Press, 2015).

6. Seymour Papert, "Hard Fun," *Bangor Daily News*, 2002, accessed April 23, 2018, http://www.papert.org/articles/HardFun.html.

Essay 5

1. Marvin Minsky, *The Emotion Machine: Commonsense Thinking, Artificial Intelligence, and the Future of the Human Mind* (New York: Simon & Schuster, 2006), 2.

2. As discussed in the introductory remarks to essay 2, Marvin had taught himself how to improvise on the piano. His specialty was making up fugues in the style of Bach. For Marvin, learning to improvise fugues was a way to study the workings of the mind. In honor of Marvin's love for music and for the piano, drawings in the following section use examples from piano playing to concretize Marvin's ideas.

Notes

Introductory Remarks to Essay 6

1. See http://illuminium.org/calculus/integral.html, running SAINT. For background, please see http://logical.ai/auai/#demos.

2. *Feedback* is a technical term; for an overview, see https://en.wikipedia.org/wiki/Feedback.

3. Alan Newell and Herbert Simon, like Minsky, were pioneers in establishing the field of AI and were professors at Carnegie Mellon University.

4. Patrick Winston and Dylan Holmes, "The Genesis Manifesto: Story Understanding and Human Intelligence," forthcoming 2018, http://courses.csail.mit.edu/6.034f/Manifesto.pdf.

Essay 6

1. Marvin Minsky, *The Emotion Machine: Commonsense Thinking, Artificial Intelligence, and the Future of the Human Mind* (New York: Simon & Schuster, 2006), 271–275.

2. For discussions about making robots cooperate, see examples at http://www.cs.cmu.edu/~robosoccer/main/, http://en.wikipedia.org/wiki/Flocking_(behavior), and http://www.lalena.com/AI/Flock/.

3. See https://inventiveminds.xyz/essay6/links.

4. See Patrick Henry Winston's Introductory Remarks to Essay 6, page 121 of this volume.

5. Marvin also lists "Experimenting with 'Rule-Based Systems'" as a category of project ideas but does not elaborate.

Afterword

1. Marvin Minsky, unpublished work, c. 1993.

Further Reading

Recommended by Alan Kay

Abelson, Harold, and Andrea A. DiSessa. *Turtle Geometry: The Computer as a Medium for Exploring Mathematics*. Cambridge, MA: MIT Press, 1992.

Bruner, Jerome. *Man a Course of Study* (Occasional Paper no. 3, Social Studies Curriculum Program). Cambridge, MA: Educational Development Center, 1965.

Bruner, Jerome. *The Relevance of Education*. New York: WW Norton, 1971.

Bruner, Jerome. *Toward a Theory of Instruction*. Cambridge, MA: Belknap Press, 1966.

Dewdney, A. Kee. *The Tinkertoy Computer*. New York: Freeman, 1993.

Dow, Peter B. *Schoolhouse Politics: Lessons from the Sputnik Era*. Bridgewater, NJ: Replica Books, 2000.

Grey Walter, William. "An Imitation of Life." *Scientific American* 182, no. 5 (1950): 42–45.

Grey Walter, William. *The Living Brain*. New York: Norton, 1953.

Grey Walter, William. "A Machine That Learns." *Scientific American* 185, no. 2 (1951): 60–63.

Hebb, Donald O. *The Organization of Behavior: A Neuropsychological Theory*. New York: Routledge, 2012.

Hillis, W. Daniel. *The Pattern on the Stone: The Simple Ideas That Make Computers Work*. New York: Basic Books, 2015.

Kahneman, Daniel. *Thinking, Fast and Slow*. New York: Farrar, Straus and Giroux, 2015.

Kandel, Eric R., and Sarah Mack. *Principles of Neural Science*. New York: McGraw-Hill Medical, 2014.

Kay, Alan. "Adele Goldberg, Personal Dynamic Media." *IEEE Computer*, March 1977.

Kay, Alan C. "Microelectronics and the Personal Computer." *Scientific American* 237, no. 3 (September 1977): 231–245.

Kay, Alan C. "Computers, Networks and Education." *Scientific American* 265, no. 3 (September 1991): 138–149.

Kay, Alan C., and Adele Goldberg. "Personal Dynamic Media." *Computer* 10, no.3 (March 1977): 31–41.

Macauley, David. *Building the Book Cathedral*. Boston: Houghton Mifflin, 1999.

Macaulay, David. *Cathedral*. Boston: Houghton Mifflin, 1973.

Minsky, Marvin. "Form and Content in Computer Science." *Journal for the Association of Computing Machinery* 17, no. 2 (April 1970). http://web.media.mit.edu/~minsky/papers/TuringLecture/TuringLecture.html.

Minsky, Marvin. "Preface." In *LogoWorks: Challenging Programs in Logo*, edited by Cynthia Solomon, Margaret Minsky, and Brian Harvey, vii–xii. New York: McGraw-Hill, 1986.

Minsky, Marvin L. *Computation: Finite and Infinite Machines*. Taipei: Central Book Co, 1967.

Minsky, Marvin. *The Society of Mind*. New York: Simon & Schuster Paperbacks, 2007.

Papert, Seymour. *Mindstorms: Children, Computers, and Powerful Ideas.* New York: Basic Books, 1980.

Papert, Seymour. "Teaching Children to Be Mathematicians versus Teaching about Mathematics." *International Journal of Mathematical Education in Science and Technology* 3, no. 3 (1972): 249–262. doi:10.1080/0020739700030306.

Papert, Seymour, and Cynthia Solomon. "Twenty Things to Do with a Computer." Artificial Intelligence Memo no. 248 and Logo Memo no. 3, AI Laboratory, MIT, June 1971.

Silverman, Brian. Logo MicroWorlds Ex Vocabulary. Logo Computer Systems Inc., 2003–2004. http://www.lcsi.ca/pdf/microworldsex/microworlds-ex-vocabulary.pdf.

Solomon, Cynthia. *Computer Environments for Children: A Reflection on Theories of Learning and Education.* Cambridge, MA: MIT Press, 1986.

Travers, M. "Agar: An Animal Construction Kit." Master's thesis, MIT Media Laboratory, 1988.

Travers, M. "Programming with Agents: New Metaphors for Thinking about Computation." PhD diss., MIT Media Laboratory, 1996.

Wiener, Norbert. *Cybernetics: Or Control and Communication in the Animal and the Machine.* 2nd ed. Cambridge, MA: MIT Press, 1961.

Recommended by Gary Stager

Duckworth, Angela. *Grit: The Power of Passion and Perseverance.* Toronto: Collins, 2016.

Duckworth, Angela L., Christopher Peterson, Michael D. Matthews, and Dennis R. Kelly. "Grit: Perseverance and Passion for Long-Term Goals." *Journal of Personality and Social Psychology* 92, no. 6 (2007): 1087–1101. doi:10.1037/0022-3514.92.6.1087.

Dweck, Carol. "Even Geniuses Work Hard." *Educational Leadership* 68, no. 1 (2010): 16–20.

Dweck, Carol. *Mindset: The New Psychology of Success*. New York: Random House, 2006.

Dweck, Carol S. "Mindsets and Human Nature: Promoting Change in the Middle East, the Schoolyard, the Racial Divide, and Willpower." *American Psychologist* 67, no. 8 (2012): 614–622.

Lave, Jean, and Etienne Wenger. *Situated Learning: Legitimate Peripheral Participation*. Cambridge, UK: Cambridge University Press, 1991.

Papert, Seymour. *The Children's Machine: Rethinking School in the Age of the Computer*. New York: BasicBooks, 2000.

Papert, Seymour. "Hard Fun." *Bangor Daily News*, 2002. Accessed February 12, 2018. http://www.papert.org/articles/HardFun.html.

Piaget, Jean. *Science of Education and the Psychology of the Child*. New York: Orion Press, 1970.

Sarason, Seymour Bernard. *And What Do You Mean by Learning?* Portsmouth, NH: Heinemann, 2004.

Sarason, Seymour Bernard. *The Predictable Failure of Educational Reform: Can We Change Course before Its Too Late?* San Francisco: Jossey-Bass, 1991.

Sarason, Seymour Bernard. *Revisiting the Culture of School and the Problem of Change*. New York: Teachers College Press, 1996.

Sarason, Seymour Bernard. *A Self-Scrutinizing Memoir*. New York: Teachers College Press, 2003.

Vygotskiĭ, L. S., Michael Cole, Sally Stein, and Allan Sekula. *Mind in Society: The Development of Higher Psychological Processes*. Cambridge, MA: Harvard University Press, 1978.

Vygotsky, Lev. *Thought and Language*. Edited and translated by Eugenia Hanfmann, Gertrude Vakar, and Alex Kozulin. Revised and expanded ed. Cambridge, MA: MIT Press, 2012.

Index

Page numbers in italic refer to figures.

Abelson, Hal, xxiv, 37
Abilities, 109–110
Actions, purposeful or goal-based, 135
Adams, Curt, 74–75
AI Lab (MIT), xix–xx, xxv
AI Lab (MIT) Logo Group, xxii, xxiv, xxvi
Algebra, abstract, 50
Ambitions, acquiring, 90–95
Analogies, finding appropriate, 111
Apple Logo, xxii
Apprenticeships, 53–54
ArcMac, xxv
Aristotle, 92
Arithmetic
  magic of, 4
  questions children should ask about, 48
  teaching, xxvii, 4, 41–42, 44–45

Artificial intelligence (AI). *See also* "Education and Psychology" (Minsky)
  architecture, xxxii
  background, xv, 130
  existential risks of, xxxv
  founding principles, xxxii
  key insights of, xxxvii
  pursuing, reasons for, xxxvii–xxxviii
  social nature of, xxxv
Atari Cambridge Research Lab, xxii–xxiii, xxiv, xxvi
Atari Logo, xxii, xxv, 16
Athletics, 115
Attachment figures, 78, 92
Augustine, 137

BBN Technologies, xix
Behavior-based theories, 131–140
Bender, Walter, xxv, 99
Bontá, Paula, xxv

Brains, human. *See also* Minds
  compositional quality, xxxiv
  resources of, 105
Bruner, Jerome, 62
Bullying, 95, 117

Celebrities, emulating, 88–89
Chess-playing machine, 71
Childhood
  carefree, 66–67, 88
  playfulness of, 104
Children
  ambitions, acquiring, 90–95
  attention spans, 68
  bullying, 95, 117
  cognitive styles, diversity in, 72–74
  development of, grade-based segregation and, 65–67
  goals, acquiring, 90–95
  infantile attitudes, 65–66
  intellectual, predicaments of, 117–118
  interests, helping to pursue, 94–95
  limitations, teaching, 81–83
  preparing for the future, 53–55, 73
  as programmed computers, 81–83, 86–87
  resourcefulness, 85
  self-image in, 87–90, 141
  socializing, 74–75
  typical, 72–74
Cognitive maps, 81
Cognitive science, 130

Cognitive styles, 72–74
Cognitive towers, 99, 105–106
Combinatorics, 50
Common sense, 123
Competence, 130
Computer literacy, 3
Computers
  abilities of, 12–13
  compositional quality, xxxiv
  in education, role of, xxxvii
  explaining, 4
  limitations of, 25
  personal, precursors to, 30–34
  as potentially human, xxxvii
  potential of, xxxi–xxxii
  programmed, children as, 81–83, 86–87
  promise of, 18
  TinkerToy, xxiv–xxv, 9, 30–31
  understanding, 10–11
Computer science
  in the curriculum, 142
  importance of, 167n1
  Minsky on, xv
Computer science education, xxiii
Confessions (Augustine), 137
Constructing Modern Knowledge, xxiv, 60–61
Constructionism, xxxvi, 140–141
Construction sets. *See also specific sets*
  limitations of, 10
  magic of, 5, 16
  pre-purposing, success and, 25
Crafts, physical fabrication, 115
Creativity, xxxvi

Index

Critical thinking, learning, 151
Critics, 107–109
Curriculum
  computer science in the, 142
  cybernetics in the, 140–142
  psychology in the, 128–130
  school structure and, 62
Cybernetics
  background, 143
  feedback loops, systems with, 142–144
  founding principles, xxxii
  inspiration from, 23–24, 130
  projects, 144–151
  psychology and, 130
  teaching, instead of psychology, 140–144
  working models of intelligence and, 23–24

Debugging, 100–101
Discomfort, enjoying, 137–138
Division, 46
Draw, learning to, 155–162
Dropouts, 89–90

Edtech, 101
Education
  computer science in, 142
  computers in, role of, xxxvii
  cybernetics in, 140–142
  "Effects of Grade-Based Segregation" (Minsky), 59, 65, 134
  maker movement, 99–100
  psychology in, 128–130

"Questioning General Education" (Minsky), xxxvi, 99, 103
  standard model, limitations of, xxxvi
"Education and Psychology" (Minsky), 127
  introduction, 121
  on self-reflection, xxxvi
  theme, xxxii
"Effects of Grade-Based Segregation" (Minsky), 65
  on cognition, 134
  introduction, 59
Efforts, mindless, xxxiii
Emotion Machine, The (Minsky), xiii, xv, xxx, xxxii, 71–72, 79, 84–85, 88, 91, 94, 99–101, 105–107, 113
Emotion-reason-aesthetics, distinctions among, 79
Emotions, 137–140, 172n1
Erector-Sets, 9, 116
Evolution, understanding, 17
Expertise
  developing, 104–105
  diverse, 60
  Minsky's early areas of, 155–162, 174n2
  negative, 57, 94, 112, 130

Fabrications
  computational, 116–117
  simulated, 116
Failure, 94, 109, 139
Failures, academic, 89–90
Fake news, 124

Feedback, 122
Feedback loops, systems with, 142–144
Feelings, 77, 137–140, 172n1
Feurzeig, Wally, xix
FischerTechnik, 10
50-minute hour, 68–72
Force-sensing screens, xxii
Four-voice music box, xviii, xx
Freud, Sigmund, xviii, 113
Fry, Stephen, 77
Fugue, 37
  defined, 170n1
  improvising, 174n2
Fun, hard, 25, 61, 101

Games, teaching with, 42
Gears, magic in, 78
Geeks, 95, 117
General Problem Solver (GPS), xxxii, 135–136, 142
General Turtle, xxi
Genesis Project, xxv–xxvi
Genius, xxix
Geometry, 46, 48
Goals
  achieving, 109–110
  acquiring, 90–95
  centrality of, xxxii–xxxiii
  developing, social processes in, xxxiv
  internalizing in education, xxxii
  process-based, 142–143
  thinking and, 135
GP, programming language, 27–28
GPS. *See* General Problem Solver (GPS)

Grey Walter. *See* Walter, William Grey
Grit, 89

Hard fun, 25, 61, 101
Heuristics, reflexive, xxxvi–xxxvii
Hillis, Danny, xxiv–xxv, 30
Hobbies
  education vs., 104–105
  flat, 114
  focusing on, 106
  mathematic concepts, thinking about, 114
  Minsky on, 61
  parental focus on, 104
  vertical specialties vs., 114–116
Honesty, intellectual, 25
Hour of Code, 100

Ideas
  developing, 68–69
  powerful, learning, 20, 22
  power of, xxxi–xxxii
If->Do rules, 134–135
If->Do->Then rules, 135
Impersonation, 85
Imprimers
  defined, xxxv, 92
  internalized copies of, 78–79
  "Learning from Role Models, Mentors, and Imprimers" (Minsky), xxix, xxxii, 77, 81
  for value acquisition, 93
"Infinite Construction Kit, The" (Minsky), 3
  afterword, 19

Index

quotes, 77
secret of, xxxiii
Intelligence
  fixed, 132–133
  importance of, 66
  model component, 78
  term usage, 109–110
  working models of, 23–24

Joystick, force-feedback, xxii

Kay, Alan, xxii, xxiii–xxiv, 19
Knowledge
  same-level, 114
  social construction of, 60
Kubrick, Stanley, 157, 162

Language
  learning, 3
  of mathematics, 52–53
Laptops, precursors to, 30–34
Lave, Jean, 60
Learning
  by animals, 91
  diversity in, 72–74
  efficient, 71
  joyous struggles of, 25
  by making, Minsky on, 62
  negative in, 57
  playful, 101
  power of, 25
  real, 25
  reward-based, 128–130, 137–139
  social nature of, xxxv
  teaching, 127

"Learning from Role Models, Mentors, and Imprimers" (Minsky), 81
  on goals, xxxii
  introduction, 77
  on problem solving, xxix
  theme, xxxii
Learning machines, 71–72
Learning theory
  behavior-based, 131–140
  reward-based, 128–130
"Learning to Draw" (Margaret Minsky), 155
LEGO, 9–10, 116
Letters, 11
Lifelong Kindergarten Group, xxxv
Literacy, computer, 3
Literature, 11
Logic, 49
Logo
  beginnings, xix, 78, 99
  components of, 8
  compositional quality, xxxiv
  constructing from, 8
  four-voice music box, xviii, xx
  object-oriented, xxii
  possibilities of, 13
Logo Computer Systems Inc., xxi–xxii, xxv
Logo Group (AI Lab, MIT), xix, xxii, xxiv, xxvi
Logo turtle geometry, 24
Logo turtle-graphics computer, xxi–xxii
Logo turtles, programming, 27–29

LogoWriter, xxv
Lorre, Chuck, 87–90

Machines
 chess-playing, 71
 cultural prejudices against, xxxvii
 mindful, creating, xxxvii
 thinking of oneself as, 151–152
 TinkerToy computer, 9, 30–31
Magic, 124
Magic tricks, 151
Maker movement, 99–100
Martian szneech, 11
Mathematic concepts, thinking about, 114
Mathematics. *See also* Arithmetic
 bringing to life, 48–51
 dislike of, 81
 vocabulary of, 52–53
Mathematics, learning
 communities, 53–55
 difficulty of, reasons for, xxxii–xxxiii
 expertise, negative, 57
 impoverished language of, 51
 introduction, 37–40
 mentors, 53–55
 novelty over drudgery, emphasizing, 55–56
 programming for, 27, 45–46
 "What Makes Mathematics Hard to Learn" (Minsky), 41
  introduction, 37
  theme, xxxii
Mathematics curriculum, historically, 44–45
Mathematics education, improvements proposed by DOE, 171n5
McCarthy, John, xviii–xix
McCulloch, Warren, xix
Meccano, xxxiv, 9, 116
Mechanics, 49
Memory, 10, 68–69
Mental resources, 109–110
Mentors
 defined, 93
 finding in network communities, 96–97
 functions of, 94
 "Learning from Role Models, Mentors, and Imprimers" (Minsky), xxix, xxxii, 77, 81
MicroWorlds, xxv
Mindlessness, xxxvii
Mindlinking, 11
Minds. *See also* Brains, human
 cognitive towers of, 105–106
 compositional quality, xxxiv
 critics in, 107–109
 explaining, 24
 high-level credit-assignments, 132
 multiplicity of parts, xxxv–xxxvi
 preconceptions, suffering caused by, xxxviii
Mindstorms (Papert), 78
Minsky, Margaret
 background, xxvi
 "Learning to Draw," 155

Index

Minsky, Marvin
  accomplishments, xxix
  biography, xii–xiii
  characteristics, xxix–xxxi, 59, 61, 63, 122–123
  expertise, early areas of, 155–162, 174n2
  fireside chats, 60–61
  genius, xxix
  on hobbies, 61
  illustrations of, xi, xvi, 20
  inspiration, xxx
  learning, approach to, xxxi
  on learning by making, 62
  legacy, 19, 63
  Papert and, xvii–xxiii, xix
  on problem solving, 61–62
  on school structure as a curricular impediment, 62
  Solomon and, xviii–xxiii
Minsky essays
  "Education and Psychology" (essay 6), xxxii, xxxvi, 121, 127
  "Effects of Grade-Based Segregation" (essay 3), 59, 65, 134
  "The Infinite Construction Kit" (essay 1), xxxiii, 3, 19, 77
  "Learning from Role Models, Mentors, and Imprimers" (essay 4), xxix, xxxii, 77, 81
  "Questioning General Education" (essay 5), xxxvi, 99, 103
  "What Makes Mathematics Hard to Learn" (essay 2), xxxii, 37, 41

Minsky essay themes
  goals, centrality of, xxxii–xxxiii
  multiplicity, xxxv–xxxvi
  networks as escape, xxxv
  other minds, xxxiv–xxxviii
  parts, construction from, xxxiii–xxxiv
  problem solving, xxxvi
  reflection, centrality of, xxxvi–xxxvii
  summary overview, xxxvii–xxxviii
Mistakes, 57
MIT Media Lab, xxiii, xxiv, xxxv
MIT programming course 6.001, xxiv
Modeling, computation providing, xxxvii
Montessori, Maria, 21
Multiplication table, 41–42
Multiplicity, xxxv–xxxvi
Music, composing, 114
Music box, xviii, xx
"Music Mind, and Meaning" (Minsky), 79
"My not I" thinking, 124, 152

Naming, 121–122
Negroponte, Nicholas, xxiii, xxv
Nerds, 95, 117–118
Networks
  as escape, xxxv
  finding mentors in, 96–97
Newell, Allen, 71, 90, 122, 135
Nicomachean Ethics (Aristotle), 92
Note-taking, 70

Novelty over drudgery,
  emphasizing, 55–56
Numbers
  counting, 4
  magic of, 77

One Laptop per Child (OLPC),
  xxiii, xxv, xxxi, xxxv
Oppenheimer, Robert, 61
Other minds
  introduction, xxxiv–xxxviii
  multiplicity, xxxv–xxxvi
  networks as escape, xxxv
  reflection, centrality of,
    xxxvi–xxxvii

Papert, Artemis, xxv
Papert, Seymour, xii–xiv, xvi–xxiii,
  xvii, *xx*, xxxvii, 8, 23–25, 32–
  33, 59–62, 78, 81, 99–100, 109,
  116–117, 122, 140, 156
Papert's principle, xviii
Parts, construction from, xxxiii–
  xxxiv, 12–17
Perceptrons (Minsky & Papert),
  156–162
Personal computers, precursors to,
  30–34
Physics, 46
Piaget, Jean, xvii–xviii, xix, 60
Piano, xxvi, 62, 174n2
Play
  hard fun, 25, 61, 101
  work vs., 21, 67
Plays, composing, 114
PlayStation of the future, xxii

Pleasure, 94, 137–140
Pólya, George, 103
Problem solving
  abilities, talents, and mental
    resources in, 109–110
  analogies, finding appropriate,
    111
  critics in, 107–109
  debugging in, 100–101
  methods of, 84–87, 108
  Minsky on, 61–62
  negative expertise in, 112
  nonstandard, xxxvi
  real-world, 103
  representations, selecting
    appropriate, 111
  reward-based, 132
  self-models, constructing
    realistic, 112–113
  specialties, horizontal vs.
    vertical, 114–117
Programming
  introducing, 124
  learning, 100
  learning mathematics through,
    27, 45–46
  storytelling and, 124
Programming languages,
  compositional quality, xxxiv
Programs
  advantages over construction
    sets, 10
  are societies, 12–18
  magic of, 4–5, 16
  Turing on, 13–14
Psychology

Index

"Education and Psychology" (Minsky), xxxii, xxxvi, 121, 127
  in the primary school curriculum, 128–130
  teaching cybernetics instead of, 140–144

"Questioning General Education" (Minsky), 103
  introduction, 99
  on multiplicity, xxxvi

Reasoning
  commonsense, 123
  teaching, 127
Recipe following, 123
Reflection
  centrality of, xxxvi–xxxvii
  in learning theory, 131
  in problem solving, 85
  self-conscious, 91
Representations, selecting appropriate, 111
Resignation, 85
Resnick, Mitchel, xxv
Resourcefulness, 113
Reward-based learning, 128–130, 137–139
Robots, projects with
  balancing and manipulation, 146
  cognition and reasoning, 149
  critical thinking, learning, 151
  expert systems, 150
  finite-state machines, 149–150
  Meccano sets, 9
  optimization and problem solving, 147
  performance systems, 148
  puzzles and game-playing, 149
  simulated vs. physical, 146
  visual recognition, 148
  voices and sound processing, 148
  walking, 144–145
Role models
  athletes as, 115
  "Learning from Role Models, Mentors, and Imprimers" (Minsky), xxix, xxxii, 77, 81
Roomba, 29
Rumplestiltskin principle, 122

Sahlberg, Pasi, 101
Schools
  Finnish, 101
  goals for, 127
  purpose of, 81
School structure, 62, 68–72
Science, understanding, 17
Scratch, xxv, xxxiv, xxxv
Segregation, grade-based
  child development and, 65–67
  cognitive styles and, 72–74
  50-minute hour, 68–72
  justification for, 60, 65
  present-day, 60
  socialization and, 74–75
Self-image, 87–90, 141, 152
Self-models, constructing realistic, 112–113

Self-reflection, xxxvi–xxxvii, 132, 152
Shame, 92, 115
Shannon, Claude, 30, 61
Silverman, Brian, xxiv–xxv, 16, 30, 77
Simon, Herbert A., 90, 122, 135
Simulations, 15–16, 116, 124
Sketchpad, 30–33
Slagle, James, 121
Smalltalk, xxiii–xxiv
Socialization, grade-based segregation and, 74–75
Society of Mind, The (Minsky), xiii, xv, xxx, xxxii, 24, 137
Solomon, Cynthia, xviii–xxiii, *xx*, *xxi*, 32–33, 99–100
SOM. See *Society of Mind, The* (Minsky)
Sound
  four-voice music box, xviii, xx
  music, composing, 114
Specialists, 94
Specialties, horizontal vs. vertical, 114–117
Sports, team-based, 115
Stager, Gary, xxiv, 59
Star Trek, 77
Statistics, 49–50
Stories, composing, 114
Storytelling, 123–125
Students
  ideas, developing, 68–69
  Minsky on, xxxi
  note-taking, 70
Success, rewarding, 132
Suffering, 138

Sung, Phil, 44
Sussman, Gerald, xxiv, 118, 122
Sutherland, Ivan, 30, 32–33
System parts, 24

Tablets, precursors to, 30–34
Talents, 109–110
Teachers, good, xxxiii
Teaching, Minsky on, xxvii
TEM. See *Emotion Machine, The* (Minsky)
Thinkers, internalizing, 19
Thinking
  computational ways of, power of, xxxvii
  developing new ways of, 132
  goal-directed, 135
  good, 127
  learning about, 121
  with "my not I," 124, 152
  new ways of, developing, xxxvi
  predicting, comparing, and planning in, 134–135
  of self as computer, xxxvii
  self-critical, 105, 118–119
  skillful, xxxiii
  about ways to think, 84–87
Thinking about thinking, 132–134. *See also* Reflection, centrality of
  feeling as a complement to, 77
  ideas learned by, 121–122
  introduction, 37–40
  learning good ways for, xxvii
  without thinking about thinking about something, xvi, 81–82
  about ways to think, 84–87

Index

Thorndike, Edward L., 128
Tic-tac-toe computer, xxiv–xxv, 9, 30
Tigers, 11
TinkerToys
  benefits of, xxxiv
  components of, 4–6, *6*, 21
  computers from, xxiv–xxv, 9, 30–31
  creating structures from, 5–7
  limits, 30
  parts, construction from, 21–23, *21*, *22*, *23*, 24–25, *26*
Topology, 50
Tortoises, 23–24, 27. *See also* Walter, William Grey; Turtles
Travers, Mike, xxvi, xxix, 19
Turing, Alan, 13–16
TurtleArt, xxv
Turtles
  beginnings, xix–xx
  display, xix–xx
  floor, xix–xx
  robot, 23–24, 27
"20 Things to Do with a Computer" (Papert & Solomon), 99
2001: A Space Odyssey, 157, 162

Values, acquiring, 91–93
Van Loon, Henrik, 157
Vector graphics, xxi–xxii
Von Neumann, John, 61
Vygotsky, Lev, 60

Walter, William Grey, 23–24, 27–28
Wenger, Etienne, 60
"What Makes Mathematics Hard to Learn" (Minsky), 41
  introduction, 37
  on answering questions, xxxii
  theme, xxxii
Winston, Patrick H., xxv–xxvi, 28, 121
Words, 11
Work vs. play, 21, 66–67
Worry, 3

Xiao Xiao, xxvi–xxvii

www.ingramcontent.com/pod-product-compliance
Lightning Source LLC
Chambersburg PA
CBHW030650230426
43665CB00011B/1025